The Calendar Question

The Calendar Question

By Reverend Basile Sakkas

Edited by Subdeacon Nektarios Harrison, M.A.

Orthodox Traditionalist Publications

Washington, D.C.

2024

Original Publishing 1973
ISBN: 979-886-224-2850

www.orthodoxtraditionalist.com

Assistant Editor: Maria Spanos, B.A.

"Therefore, brethren, stand fast and hold the traditions which you were taught, whether by word or our epistle."

2nd Thessalonians 2:15

Table of Contents

Saint Philaret of New York (1903-1985)

Introduction

The Holy Apostle commands us saying, "Hold fast the traditions which ye have received, whether by word of mouth or through an epistle of ours." (2 Thes. 11:15). It is therefore with genuine joy that we recommend to you this present study written by a Greek brother, Fr. Basil Sakkas, who is a priest under our Synod of the Russian Orthodox Church Outside of Russia serving in Geneva, Switzerland. It is the voice of a true Orthodox Christian of the Greek Church, which Church has been afflicted for the last fifty years with divisions, and contention, and persecution on account of the innovation of the New Calendar which was brought about in 1924 by modernists in a hasty and most uncanonical manner.

Fr. Basil sets forth in a clear fashion the reasons why many of our Greek Orthodox brethren refused to follow after the uncanonical change of the calendar in their Church in 1924 and, being aided by the fathers of the Holy Mountain Athos, courageously and justly withstood this innovation which was the beginning of an inundation of innovations perpetuated by the modernists until the sorry state in which we are found today of the heresy of Ecumenism.

All serious and concerned Orthodox Christians should pay attention to this work of Fr. Basil, especially today when there is talk by the modernists of changing the Orthodox *Paschalia*. The translation and printing of this study is especially precious since the texts of the three condemnations of the Gregorian Calendar enacted by Pan-Orthodox councils in the 16th Century and the Pan-Orthodox condemnation of modernism last century presided over by Patriarch Anthemus appear for the first time in English.

These condemnations were never lifted by any later council—they still stand and are binding for all Orthodox Christians. The innovation of the New Calendar brought about schism in all the local churches that adopted it. Thus, Greece, Cyprus, Rumania, and now Bulgaria have tasted the fruits of disobedience. It is only to be regretted that the Orthodox peoples of the above-mentioned Churches were not able to all rise up together and as a great wave overcome and put down this tide of innovations, as the Russian people put down the modernism of the "Living Church" in this century. Our own Russian Church in the person of the then Archbishop Anastassy of blessed memory, later Metropolitan and the First Hierarch of our Synod, strongly and resolutely protested the innovation of the New Calendar and the other modernisms of Patriarch Meletius Metaxakis of sorry memory at the gathering in Constantinople in 1923, which is wrongly referred to as Pan-Orthodox since the Patriarchates of Alexandria and Jerusalem and the Church of Cyprus did not attend. Most hierarchs of the Church of Constantinople also refused to attend, thus protesting the uncanonicity of the forced political appointment of Meletius as Ecumenical Patriarch. The Primate of our Church at that time, Metropolitan Anthony, also protested against that reform in his correspondence with the Eastern Patriarchs and received answers supporting his stand.

"Glory and honor," therefore, in the words of the Holy Apostle, to all who hold fast to the traditions and keep the Faith as we have received it without additions or subtractions even though they be slandered and persecuted.

†Metropolitan Philaret

The 14th of April 1972
Feast of St. Martin the Confessor, Pope of Rome,
and the Bishop Confessors with him in the West.

Memorandum

To: The Most Reverend Vitaly, Archbishop of Montreal and Canada; Member of the Holy Synod of the Russian Church Outside Russia. 8011 Champagneur, Montreal 303, Que., Canada

From: Priest Basil Sakkas, under the canonical jurisdiction of the Most Reverend Anthony, Archbishop of Geneva and Western Europe; Member of the same Synod. CH 1217 Meyrin-Cite Geneva, Switzerland

Subject: The crisis of conscience which has come upon the true Orthodox Christians of Greece because of the change of the Ecclesiastical Calendar in 1924.

Most Reverend Master,

With great reverence, I kiss your venerable hand and ask humbly for your fatherly and episcopal blessing and prayers. With the blessing of my own bishop, the Most Reverend Archbishop Anthony of Geneva and Western Europe, the blessing of my spiritual father, the reverend Abbot Ambrose, head of the French Orthodox communities of the jurisdiction of the Holy Synod of the Russian Church Outside Russia, who has exhorted me since 1964 to undertake a study of the problem of the calendar, and the blessing of the most reverend Archimandrite Father Panteleimon, Abbot of the Monastery of the Holy Transfiguration of our Lord in Boston, who has given me abundant material and examined the rough draft of this present study, I dare to compile this present memorandum concerning the question of the calendar, in case this question should be examined by the Great Council of our most Holy Church, which is soon to be convoked. I address the present work to you Most Reverend Master, because, geographically, you are the hierarch closest to the Seat of the Holy

3

Synod in the New World to whom I can address myself directly in the French language. It goes without saying that this present exposition does not claim to be a dogmatical definition, neither is it set forth as a solution to the problem. Although the Chosen people of the Lord are the "guardians of the Truth," nonetheless, the definition of the dogmas and ecclesiastical tradition is the responsibility of a council of bishops. In truth, the council of hierarchs constitutes the mouth of the Church, so far as, of course, the hierarchs, the members of the council, are Orthodox, that is, that they teach no heresies which have been recognized as such by all previous Councils or by the Holy Fathers.

Since I the unworthy, as well as a great multitude of the faithful, have found in your venerable person, Most Reverend Master, "a high priest that befitteth us" (Heb. 7:26), who, concerning the subject of Orthodoxy, has given us up till now so many proofs and sureties that your teaching is more clear than crystal and that you proclaim the Holy Tradition of the Orthodox to be holy, spotless, integral, sealed by God and subject to no variation, for these reasons, then, I find within myself a filial boldness which permits me to address this present study to you.

In truth, Holy Tradition teaches that we, the priests, and deacons, are the eyes of the bishops; but the eye is only an organ of the mind. It is the duty of the mind to judge that which the eyes behold. Hence, I shall undertake to express the objections which present themselves to the consciences of hundreds of thousands of Orthodox Christians (as well as to my own conscience) as a result of the change of the calendar. If it be the case that in my zeal, my intelligence proves deficient, I am confident before the Lord that your paternal good judgment, Most Reverend Master, will make good the deficiencies in my faith and correct those points in which I might possibly be in error or where I lack precision. I do not say this by way of flattery—God forbid—but possessing the proofs of your love for the Church, a sincere love having no ulterior motives, it would be arrogance on my part to suppose that I love the Church more than you or know better how to serve Her interests. Thanks be unto God that I

4

have not yet had such a temptation, but rather I feel within myself the liberty and confidence of a son towards his father.

For quite some time I have desired to publish certain official texts from Greek sources concerning the calendar issue, which sources were unknown in the Diaspora; in these texts one can see clearly the relation of the calendar to the heresies of ecumenism and modernism which conceal themselves behind this issue, though the first seems "insignificant" to certain individuals. The approaching convocation of the Great Council of our most Holy Church, however, obliges me to put off this informative work until a later date and compose this present study in the hope that it will reach your attention, Most Reverend Master. Because of this lack of time, it has been impossible for me to resort to the primary sources which are quoted, and therefore, I hope to be pardoned if I refer simply to the different works written on this subject by those who have battled for forty-seven years for the piety of our Fathers.

I begin, therefore, my exposition, hoping in the power of Your holy prayers.

Chapter One

The Dogmatical Significance of the Ecclesiastical Calendar

Our adversaries pretend that the calendar "is not a dogma," thus leaving it to be understood that one can do with it what one pleases. Is the question of the calendar truly one of dogma? This naturally depends upon the perspective from which one examines the matter. My beard and my *rassa* certainly do not constitute a dogma, for their existence does not increase or decrease the number of the Persons of the Holy Trinity.

However, if I disdain the insignia of my ministry with which the Church of Jesus Christ has honoured me—which She regards as more precious than royal purple—will I not thus offend the Church Herself? Though my *rassa* and my beard do not in themselves constitute a dogma, yet, if I take them off without any reason, do I not dishonour the Church which has honoured me and which is the foundation of all the dogmas? How, therefore, is it possible to isolate the dogmas from the rest of the life and the experience of the Holy, Catholic and Orthodox Church of Christ?

For this reason, Synesius, the Metropolitan of Cassandria, speaking of the State (i.e., new calendar) Greek Church, says with justice: "The Greek Autocephalous Church is independent. For us, the very thought of the abolition of the celibacy of the higher clergy and the alteration of its clerical dress is very premature. Today, these two questions have nearly become dogmas and cannot be removed. Consequently, there can be no place for any official or unofficial discussion of this matter" (*Ecclesiasticos Agon*).

Thus, the dogmas are not clearly independent of the details of the daily life and acts of the Holy Church. It is nearly impossible to make a distinction between the primary and the secondary in matters of the Faith. All these things bear the sanctifying seal of the

Holy Spirit, to such a degree that we cannot touch the least matter of the Tradition without directly or indirectly disparaging the Church's dogmatic requirements.

We say this also to the modernists who undertake to make a clear distinction in the sacred canons between those which are dogmatic and those which are administrative, as if the administration and the discipline of the Church did not have the dogmas as their foundation. Thus, rendering the dogmas wholly independent of the life of the Church, these people destroy Her Theandric character and degenerate it into a moralistic idealism. Most Reverend Master, you have already clearly expressed yourself on this subject in your study of ecumenism.

Did the iconoclasts not deride the Orthodox for considering the icons, that is, boards and colours, as a dogma of the faith? Yet, who among the Orthodox of today can deny the dogmatic significance of the icons? Concerning this question, Father Paul, a monk of the Holy Sepulcher, remarked most justly that a board, before it has the countenance of our Saviour portrayed upon it, is but a common piece of wood which we may burn up or destroy. From the moment, however, that we paint the icon of Christ, the King of All, upon it, this wood becomes sanctified and a source of sanctification for us, even though the wood be of inferior quality. Likewise, the solar calendar, insofar as it is a calendar of days and months is, in itself, nothing to be esteemed. But from the moment when the Holy Church placed Her seal upon it and organized Her life upon this foundation, even though it has become astronomically erroneous, still it remains holy! The calendar is no longer Julian, but ecclesiastical, just as the board is no longer a simple piece of wood but an icon.

If we adopted the reasoning of the rationalists, we could say many things. Is it a dogma to chant the hymn "O Joyous Light" at the entrance in Vespers, or is it a dogma to make the sign of the Cross, which, as St. Basil points out, no canon prescribes? Woe unto us, if each thing about which we could say that "it is not a dogma" were rejected *ipso facto*, without reason, by some local council, after the manner of the Anglicans! Behold, therefore, why it is impossible for us to deny the dogmatic significance of the festal calendar; and we shall explain ourselves further.

A. *The Relation Between the Innovation of the New Calendar and the Heresy of Ecumenism.*

In 1920, the Ecumenical Patriarchate published an encyclical in which it recognized the assemblies of Western Christians as "fellow heirs of the grace of Christ" and openly proclaimed ecumenism as the panacea for all heresies. It adopted the change of the calendar as the first means of advancing ecumenism (this was the calendar which already had been anathematized three times by three Great Councils of the Patriarchs of the East). This encyclical, signed by the *locum tenens*, Metropolitan Dorotheus of Brusa and by eleven other metropolitans, reads, in part, as follows:

> Thus, once the sincerity and especially the confidence, has been reestablished between the Churches, we think, then, that it is necessary to rekindle and fortify the love among the Churches, esteeming one another not as strangers but, on the contrary, as kindred and as of the same household of Christ and "fellow-heirs and formed of the same body and sharing in the same promise of God in Jesus Christ" (Eph. 3:6). The different Churches, inspired by love and setting it in the foremost place in their deliberations and relations among themselves, can diminish and curtail the separation between themselves, instead of extending and augmenting it, while awakening a consistent and fraternal interest concerning the state, stability and well-being of the other Churches, by showing assiduity in giving heed to and knowing more precisely that which is occurring in them and, more precisely by extending a prompt hand of help and assistance to each other. In this way they shall accomplish and realize many good things for their own glory and profit as well as that of the entire body of Christians.

9

This amenity and beneficent disposition towards one another can manifest itself and prove itself in a more particular fashion, which, according to our opinion, should be as follows:

1. through the adoption by all the Churches of one single calendar so that the great Christian feasts may be everywhere celebrated simultaneously;

2. through the exchange of fraternal letters on the occasion of the great feasts of the ecclesiastical year, as is the custom, and on other special occasions;

3. through more fraternal relations between the representatives of the different Churches;

4. through the establishment of relations between the theological schools and the representatives of the theological science, and the exchange of theological and ecclesiastical periodicals and works published by each Church;

5. through the sending of young men from one Church to the schools of other Churches for their studies;

6. through the convocation of pan-Christian assemblies for the examination of matters of common interest to all the Churches;

7. through the dispassionate and more historical examination of the dogmatic differences from a scholarly point of view and by dissertations;

8. through the mutual respect of the practices and customs of the various Churches;

9. through reciprocal granting of houses of prayer and cemeteries for funerals and burials of the adherents of other confessions who have deceased in foreign lands;

10. through the implementation of common rules by the different confessions concerning the question of mixed marriages;

11. through a reciprocal and voluntary support of the Churches in the realm of religious edification, philanthropy and other such activities. (From the second volume of Prof. John Karmiris' work, *The Dogmatic and Symbolic Monuments of the Orthodox Catholic Church*; Graz, Austria. 1968. pp. 958-959).

Certainly, it is impossible to analyze here all the blasphemies and the apostasy of the party of the Phanar, but we see that we find ourselves in the presence of a project which had been prepared a long time in advance. Hence, the change of the festal calendar for the modernists did not have as its incentive any concern over the application of scientific exactitude, nor pressures applied from without, nor a disposition—due to weakness—for the adoption of the new calendar for the sake of facility, nor does it even constitute an act of thoughtlessness. It is far worse than this: it bears witness to doctrinal corruption and a loss of an Orthodox ecclesiastical conscience, to utter indifference and to a disposition to imitate the apostasy of the West.

If, in battling against Ecumenism, we remain indifferent to the change of the festal calendar—which change was adopted precisely for the furtherance of Ecumenism—we refuse to recognize the relation between cause and effect and we combat the evil in its final development but not at its root. Without going any further, the aforementioned document is sufficient to show that the issue of the festal calendar is of a dogmatic nature and that the new calendar must be condemned mercilessly, even as the Holy Church already did four centuries ago, foreseeing its dangerous nature and, therefore, anathematizing it on three occasions. However, this does not constitute the only proof of the dogmatic character with which the question of the change of the festal calendar was invested.

11

B. The Relation between the New Calendar and Modernism.

Following the example of that which, in Russia, was called the "Living Church," Patriarch Meletius Metaxakis (known to all as a Mason) convoked some sort of assembly which he called "Pan-Orthodox" at which five bishops presided. During the ten assemblies which came together from May 10 to June 8, 1923, the following proposals were made:

1. The change of the festal calendar so that it might coincide with the secular calendar of the west.

2. The marriage of priests after their ordination.

3. The abandonment of the clergy's rasson, beard and long hair.

4. New age requirements for the ordination of deacons, priests, and bishops.

5. New age limits for those entering the monastic life.

6. The diminution or abolition of the fasts and the divine services.

7. The diminution of the restrictions on marriage due to kinship and fewer restrictions on divorce, etc.

We see, therefore, that this is not simply a question of the festal calendar or of "13 days," but rather, we see that, from many decades before, plans had been laid to destroy the divine edifice of the Church, as it were by an explosion from within! If, therefore, we had accepted the change of the calendar in 1924, which was imposed dictatorially after the manner of a *coup d'etat* (independent of whether or not the Church can change the calendar, an aspect which we will examine further on), we would have opened the way before a deluge of modernism, and then, what would remain of our Holy Orthodoxy?

We are moved with emotion when we recall the teaching of Photius Kontoglou of blessed memory, who used to say the following: "I love a young girl, but her gait does not please me; her voice irritates me; her nose is too big; I wish her eyes were a different color, and it would be preferable if she had chestnut-brown hair. Thus, is it also in spiritual matters: I love Orthodoxy, but I do not like icon lamps that burn olive oil; I find the *rassa* and the beards obsolete; the Church should adapt Her fasts to the conditions of contemporary times and Her festal calendar should also be changed, etc., etc., etc." In the first case, as in the second, we do not love the reality. We seek, rather, to adapt the reality to the demands of our imagination, which, in actuality, is the only thing we love.

So be it! If the Church wishes to change the calendar in Her Catholicity, then let Her change the calendar, if She judges this useful and if She acts in harmony with Her Tradition and the former Councils of the Church. Why should we not then submit ourselves to such a decision? Are we greater than the Church, which, according to St. John Chrysostom is "higher than heaven?" Or shall we be "super Orthodox" and "superior to the Councils?"

Yet, what relation exists between the Catholicity of the Church, on the one hand, and the revolt of 1924 or the future "8th Ecumenical Council," on the other hand? How shall we consider the future "Council" as "Pan-Orthodox" and as an authentic mouth of the Church when:

1. The present-day patriarchs and bishops are not Orthodox, but have been sullied by heresy, having thus lost their property of being Orthodox bishops and legitimate shepherds of their flocks.

2. Not only are they not Orthodox, nor even Orthodox "liberals," but often they are the instruments of the powers of darkness and the agents of the self-proclaimed enemies of Christianity.

13

3. They do not reunite in order to combat a new heresy or some danger which threatens the Church but, on the contrary, in order to preach and reiterate all the heresies and, by the principle of *aggiornamento,* to "revise," to "reform," to "curtail" and to "add" things to the basic tenets of the holy, immaculate, and immutable Faith.

4. They shamelessly avow that not only will their "Council" not endorse those things which were ratified by the previous Ecumenical and Local Councils, but, on the contrary, it shall "review" the decisions of the former Councils, since the latter have become obsolete.

It goes without saying that such a council is a "robber council" by its very nature, and that any decision concerning the festal calendar would have no meaning for true Orthodox Christians who walk in the straight and narrow path, "following the Fathers." It is, therefore, proper that, in her book, *The Executioners of Orthodoxy,* the Abbess of the Convent of the Ascension at Kopani recalls the words of St. Athanasius the Great: "It is not recently that the canons and practices of the Church have been given to us, but rather, they have been well transmitted to us by the Fathers in certainty.

Neither has the Faith commenced in our time; nay rather, It has been transmitted to us by the Lord through His disciples" (Vol. XXV, p. 22). Dositheus, the blessed Patriarch of Jerusalem, has bequeathed us the following statement: "We do not accept a new faith, but we believe only in that which our Fathers have taught us" (*Dodecabiblus,* p. 978). One of the great teachers of the Greek nation, Athanasios of Paros, says: "True doctrine is that which differs in nothing from what the Fathers have said."

"The Fathers have spoken it and we say it also," not simply because the Fathers have said it do we repeat it passively, but having with them, a common Spirit, a common Faith, and common Hope, we perceive and understand the same things as they, and we consciously

14

confess the same things as they, without contradicting or refuting them in anything.

C. *The Calendar and the Unity of the Church. General Remarks*

We have received the tradition, that in the Liturgy, we should pray as follows: "And grant that with one mouth and one heart we may glorify and chant praises to Thine all-honoured and majestic Name, of the Father, Son and Holy Spirit, now and ever and unto the ages of ages. Amen." The Orthodox Catholic Church of Jesus Christ glorifies Her holy Head upon the earth with one mouth. It happens sometimes, to give an example—that a priest celebrates the Divine Liturgy and not one person partakes of the Sacred Mysteries (although this is an abuse and an abnormal circumstance). Nonetheless, the celebrant will proclaim: "Upright, having partaken of the divine, holy, immaculate, immortal, heavenly and life-giving, fearful Mysteries of Christ, let us worthily give thanks unto the Lord." Is this a question of "routine" or "ritualism?" In such a case, could the celebrant omit the words "Upright, having partaken" since no one in his parish had taken Communion? The answer is, NO! The Divine Apostle Paul has taught us that nothing can separate the faithful from the love of Christ which embraces them, "neither height nor depth," "neither things present nor things to come," "neither life nor death" (Rom. 8:38-39). Geographical distances, therefore, cannot separate the faithful from one another. A canonical Orthodox priest does not officiate in the name of his parish only, nor "as an isolated part of a greater whole," as Dr. Alexander Kalomiros justly emphasizes. The Divine Liturgy is not a private affair, nor simply a local parish activity, but an affair of the Catholic Church. The priest officiates in the name of the Catholic Church and sanctifies the faithful with all the grace and all the sanctification of the Catholic Church. For this reason, when he says, "Upright, having partaken" (even if he only has the church sacristan present) he neither addresses himself to those who are present, nor to his parishioners only, but to all the faithful of the Catholic Church. Hence, he does not celebrate

15

locally, but with one mouth, together with all the Church. It is for this reason also that we say the prayers for the catechumens and then dismiss them, even if in a particular parish there happen to be no catechumens (or even though—if there be catechumens—we permit them to remain for the entire Liturgy by extreme economy). Just as the whole sun is reflected in each piece of a broken mirror, so also each parish is the icon of the Catholicity of the Church. But even as the unity of the Catholic Church is not broken by height or depth (that is, by distances) according to the word of the Apostle, so also is it not broken by life nor by death.

Therefore, biological death does not separate us from the Saints nor from our brethren fallen asleep in the Lord. When we say in the Creed: "I believe in One, Holy, Catholic and Apostolic Church," we simultaneously think of the Church triumphant and the Church militant, because "whether we live or whether we die we belong to the Lord" (Rom. 14:8). For this reason the triumphant and the militant Church concelebrates "with one mouth": "Grant that, with our entrance, there be an entrance also of the holy Angels who concelebrate and glorify with us..." and in another place, "Again, we offer Thee this rational and bloodless worship... for every just spirit perfected in the Faith" and in still another place, "Calling to remembrance our all holy, immaculate, exceedingly blessed...Theotokos with all the Saints, let us commit ourselves and one another..."

We concelebrate, therefore, with the heavenly powers. Our adversaries insolently say with irony: "Do they have calendars in Heaven with little tear-off pages so that they can remember the feasts?" If they wish to be so shameless and speak with such an evil spirit, we will ask them also a question in turn: "Where does earth cease and heaven begin? Where is "above" and where "below?"

We are not rationalists, but we have received from the Holy Church that when we say that Christ is "above" this does not signify that He is not "below,"—like those of the West, who are deceived in ordaining a Vicar for Him, as if the Saviour was absent from the earth! We have received the teaching that "He is entirely below without in

16

any wise being absent from on high" (from the Liturgy of St. Basil), "being seated on high together with the Father and at the same time invisibly present among us" (from the Liturgy of St. John Chrysostom). Insofar as Christ unifies the things above with the things below, the Church says that "those on high concelebrate with those below and those below chant praises together with those on high." "Rejoice, for the things of heaven rejoice together with the earth; rejoice, for the things of earth dance together with the heavens" (from the Akathist Hymn). The worship of the Catholic Church is one, both celestial and terrestrial at the same time.

1. Liturgical Separation and Disunity.

When the visible and invisible Orthodox Church chants, "Today the Virgin giveth birth to the Lord in the cave," the new calendarists chant, "Today Christ is come to be baptized in the Jordan; today John toucheth the head of the Lord!" On the day of Theophany, the Holy Orthodox Church of Jesus Christ chants, "Today the time of the feast is at hand for us; the choirs of the Saints assemble together with us, and the angels celebrate the festival together with men... Today the sacred and stentorian feast of the Orthodox exulteth. Today the Master cometh forward to be baptized..."

The sacred texts categorically bear witness to the common concelebration of the Catholic Church of Christ, visible and invisible, militant and triumphant, earthly and heavenly. The new calendarists, however, in the midst of such universal festivity are found to be chanting the verse "Rejoice, O Egypt, thou who hast brought forth such a scion, even Macarius, who is among the blessed." How have we jumped from the Jordan to Egypt, from the Theophany to the memory of St. Macarius? This cacophony cannot be called a Church, but rather a confusion, a tower of Babel. How can we expect the Lord to give us "one heart" when we do not chant "with one mouth?" But, to put the matter more precisely, the Church has exercised this unity for nearly twenty centuries and now we the intelligent ones have

17

come along in order to destroy it. The adherents of the papal calendar doggedly exclaim: "Since the date of Pascha has not been changed, the Unity of the Orthodox has not been destroyed." We reply to them, "Brethren, we beg you, come to yourselves. Why, we ask, is liturgical unity preserved so long as we celebrate Pascha together, whereas—according to your viewpoint—it is not broken if we celebrate the Saviour's Nativity, Theophany, and Transfiguration, separately? Is it not the same Saviour and Master of all? Do we celebrate one Christ at Pascha and another at the Nativity? Is He that resurrected not the same as He that was born in the cave and Who lay in the manger for our salvation?"

That is not all. The "conservative" Orthodox who have accepted the innovation of the Western calendar cry out and shout "scandal" now that Patriarch Athenagoras and his retinue wish to change the date of Pascha. Why is it that Meletius Metaxakis and Chrysostom Papadopoulos could arbitrarily change the date of the immovable feasts and Patriarch Athenagoras cannot change the *Triodion* and the *Pentecostarion* by the same principle? Athenagoras is, alas, consistent; those who are inconsistent are the "conservative" new calendarists.

2. Separation and Disunity in the Fasts.

As is known, after the Sunday of Holy Pentecost, we celebrate the Sunday of All Saints. During all the days of this week neither fasting or prostrations are permitted because of the Church's joy at the descent of the Holy Spirit. Since, for a whole week—"Bright Week"—we celebrate the feast of the Resurrection of the Saviour from the dead, the Holy Church decided to celebrate the feast of Pentecost also for a whole week, thus proclaiming to all that the Holy Spirit is equal in honor with the other Persons of the Holy Trinity.

As is also known, according to St. George of Pisidia: "The all venerable day of the feast of the life-creating Resurrection of our Lord Jesus Christ, the true God, fluctuates between March 22 and April 25. It is celebrated neither on or before March 21 nor on or after April

26." According to the date of its celebration, Pascha is called "early" or "late." If Pascha is "early," the date of the Sunday of All Saints is distant from that of the feast of Sts. Peter and Paul (June 29). If, on the other hand, Pascha is "late," the Sunday of All Saints is closer to the feast of the Holy Apostles Peter and Paul. The period between the Sunday of All Saints and the feast of the Holy Apostles is the period of the fast of the Holy Apostles.

Now, if Pascha falls on April 25, the Sunday of All Saints falls on June 20; consequently, the fast of the Apostles lasts eight days (this will be the case, for example, for Pascha of 1983). But if, on the other hand, Pascha falls on 22 March, the Sunday of All Saints falls on 17 May and the duration of the fast of the Apostles is 42 days. This fast, therefore, varies between 8 and 42 days in length. In 1725, Jeremy III, Patriarch of Constantinople was dethroned because he wished to stabilize the period of this fast to a length of 12 days. In 1783, Patriarch Callinicus of Constantinople underwent the same for wishing to stabilize this period to a length of 7 days.

But what happens with the new calendarists? When Pascha falls on April 25, their own calendar reads May 8 (already Tradition is transgressed, but let us continue). Consequently, the Sunday of All Saints falls on July 3, that is, four days *after* the feast of the Holy Apostles Peter and Paul, which, in turn falls on the Wednesday of Pentecost! As a result, the fast of the Holy Apostles is abolished. Yet, because of the fact that this fast is a tradition of the Church of very ancient origin, in the year 1929—to give an example of the ensuing confusion—the new calendarists invented a fast... during the week of Pentecost (when no fasting is permitted, for the same reason that fasting is not permitted during the week after Pascha)!

As Father Eugene Tombros, Archpriest, correctly observes: "The simultaneous, uniform and unified celebration of the feasts by Christians was overthrown." In reality, the 56th Canon of the Sixth Ecumenical Council ordains: "...it has seemed good that the Church of God, which is found throughout the entire earth, observe the fasts following one order" (*taxis*). The new calendarists have enacted

19

other things also. At the moment when the Catholic Church of Christ is well in the midst of the fast of the Nativity of our Saviour, they already are celebrating the feast itself. Thus, some fast and do works of repentance, while others make festival and rejoice. We ask ourselves, therefore, whether the divine Apostle would agree with this when he commands us, "be ye perfectly joined together in the same mind and in the same opinion" (1 Cor. 1:10). But why should we have recourse to Sacred Scripture when common sense is enough to supply us with a proper reply to this state of affairs: Is it reasonable and normal that, when the church is in the midst of fasting and preparation, the new calendarists should depart from the life and rhythm of the Church in order to concelebrate the feast with Lutherans and Calvinists?

When did the Holy Spirit descend upon the Apostles? When "they were all with one accord in one place" (Acts 2:1). It does not say "half the apostles arrived today and the other half thirteen days later." We see also in the Old Testament what God says concerning the prescribed feasts: "Every congregation of the sons of Israel shall do this" (Ex. 12:14). "Every congregation" and not each man when or as he pleases. Was the calendar of the Hebrews scientifically more exact than the so-called "Julian" calendar?

3. Concerning the Unity of the Church.

At this point, we wish to quote several sayings of the Holy Fathers concerning the unity of the Church, using the important work of the theologian, Stavros Karamitsos-Gambroulias, as our source:

From St. Irenaeus of Lyons:

As we have already said, the Church, although She be dispersed throughout the world—yet, as it were dwelling in one house, has received this *kerygma*[1] and this Faith, and She guards It carefully and believes these things, as though She had one

---

[1]   The preaching, declaration, or proclamation of the Faith.

soul and one heart; and with one voice, She preaches, teaches, and transmits these things as though She possessed one body.

From St. Ignatius the God-Bearer:
One prayer, one supplication, one mind, one hope in love and in blameless joy which is Jesus Christ, concerning which there is nothing better; ye all hasten together as it were into one temple of God, as it were to one altar.

From St. Justin the Philosopher and Martyr:
Though the number of the members be many, yet the body is called and is one; so also, is it with the assembly of the Church, for although the men be many in number, all are called and addressed by one name, as though they were one. They are as ones having one soul, one assembly and one Church.

We shall end this present chapter, which was entitled "The Dogmatical Significance of the Calendar" by quoting His Holiness, Photius, the Patriarch of Alexandria, who in his document No. 226 of April 20, 1924, asks the following concerning the change of the festal calendar: "How could it (the change) be considered foreign to dogmatical and canonical considerations and conditions?"

With God's assistance and by Your holy prayers, I shall begin the second chapter.

Chapter Two

The Festal Calendar as a Tradition of the Church

Introduction

If, previous to 1924, the Church had not taken a position on the calendar issue, it would have been possible to accept discussion on this subject. However, the Church had taken into consideration the arguments of Her adversaries well before this time and was quite aware of the astronomical deficiencies of Her calendar; yet, even so, She steadfastly refused to change. The Church did not simply express an opinion or leave the question as a *theologoumenon*[2], but rather, She took a definite position, not only forbidding the use of the papal calendar but even anathematizing it by Pan-Orthodox Councils. Therefore, how can we, without any valid reason, and without violating Tradition, return to this question which has already been examined by the Church, and upon which She has already pronounced Her verdict?

A. *The Condemnation of the Papal New Calendar.*

The very man who changed the calendar, the Archbishop of Athens, Chrysostom Papadopoulos, admitted that the Gregorian Calendar had been condemned thrice, saying, "Jeremy II, together with Sylvester of Alexandria in 1583, and then with Sophronius of Jerusalem in 1587, made a declaration against the Gregorian calendar and later convoked the Great Council of 1593, in which Meletius Pegas, the Patriarch of Alexandria, also participated" (A Critical Study of the Condemnation of the Calendar). Sacred Scripture teaches us that David cut off the head of Goliath with Goliath's own sword; and for this very reason have we set forth the confession of the innovating Archbishop.

---

[2] A debatable theological doctrine.

1. *The First Condemnation of the New Calendar in 1583*

In the work *Ecclesiastical History*, written by Metropolitan Meletius of Athens (published in Austria, 1784. Ch. XI, p. 402) we read:

> The Council of Jerusalem convoked because of the new calendar. During the reign of the same Patriarch Jeremy, a Council of Metropolitans was convoked in Constantinople in 1583, with Sylvester, Patriarch of Alexandria, also being in attendance. This Council condemned the calendar which had been introduced by Gregory of Rome, and did not accept it, as the Latins had requested.

According to the Codex Manuscript (#772) of the Russian Monastery of St. Panteleimon on Mt. Athos, we learn of the *sigillium*[3] issued by this Council:

> The *sigillium* of the Patriarchal Encyclical to the Orthodox Christians in every land commands them under the penalty of punishment and anathema not to accept the new *Paschalion*[4] or the new calendar but to remain with that which was well defined once and for all by the 318 Holy and God-bearing Fathers of the First Ecumenical Council.

In the year of the God-Man, 1583.
12th Indiction. November 20
The Patriarch of Constantinople Jeremy II
The Patriarch of Alexandria Sylvester
The Patriarch of Jerusalem Sophronius
and the other hierarchs of the Council who were present.

---

[3] An official decree, bearing the Patriarchal seals.

[4] The system of reckoning the date of Pascha.

2. The Second Condemnation of the New Calendar in 1587.

In the *Ecclesiastical History* (Constantinople 1912. Vol. III. p. 125), written by Philaret Baphides, Metropolitan of Didymotichon, we read a confirmation of the condemnation of 1583 and moreover: "Likewise in 1587, a council at Constantinople was convoked where, in the presence of Jeremy II, Meletius Pegas and Sophronius of Jerusalem, the correction of the calendar was condemned as being perilous and unnecessary and as being, rather, the cause of many dangers."

3. The Third Condemnation of the New Calendar in 1593.

This Council took place in February 1593, in the Holy Church of the Mother of God of Consolation. In its Eighth Canon, it prescribes the following concerning the change of the calendar:

> Concerning the rejection of the new calendar, that is, the innovation of the Latins regarding the celebration of Pascha. We wish that that which has been decreed by the Fathers concerning Holy and Salutary *Pascha* remain unshaken...Let all those who have dared to transgress the definitions regarding the Holy Feast of the Salutary Pascha be excommunicated and rejected from the Church of Christ.

> The Patriarch of Constantinople Jeremy II
> The Patriarch of Antioch Joachim
> The Patriarch of Jerusalem Sophronius
> The Patriarch of Alexandria Meletius

According to Polycarp, Bishop of Diaulia (Cf. *The Change of the Calendar.* Athens, 1947. p. 13) "...in 1593, a Council of the Orthodox Churches was convoked at Constantinople where the four patriarchs, the plenipotentiary of the Russian Church and many other Orthodox hierarchs representing the Orthodox Churches participated.

25

This Council reiterated the excommunication of the Most Holy Patriarch Jeremy II and issued an encyclical which, among other things, stated the following:

> He that does not follow the customs of the Church which were decreed by the Seven Holy Ecumenical Councils which have ordained well that we observe the Holy Pascha and the *Menologion*[5], and wishes to follow the new *Paschalia* and *Menologion* of the Pope's astronomers, and, opposing himself to all these things, wishes to overturn and destroy them, let him be anathema and outside of the Church of Christ and the assembly of the faithful..."

B. The Steadfast Rejection of the Gregorian Calendar on the Part of the Orthodox Church throughout the Centuries.

The refusal to adopt the Gregorian calendar constitutes a long tradition of the Church which we cannot transgress impuniously— unless we accept the supposition that the Church has acted due to "ignorance" or simply out of a "reactionary spirit" for so many centuries in Her persistent refusal and rejection of this cancerous growth.

1. From ancient times, the Church has been aware of the calendar's imperfection. For this reason, She fixed a conventional equinox which disregards the astronomical equinox.
2. In 1324, Nicephorus Gregoras determined the calendar's error with exactness and submitted a report containing propositions for changing it; however, nothing came of this.
3. In 1371, the monk Isaacius and Matthew Blastaris approved Gregoras' calendar and supported it, but the

---

5   The Calendar of immovable feasts.

Church showed no interest.

4. During the days shortly before the fall of Constantinople, George Gemistus proposed new reforms for the calendar, which were likewise rejected by the Church.

5. In 1582, Patriarch Jeremy II wrote a letter to the Orthodox Church of Poland, forbidding the use of the new calendar, under the penalty of excommunication.

6. In 1582, Patriarch Jeremy II wrote a letter to the Doge of Venice, wherein he shows that the question of the calendar is a matter lacking in seriousness: "child's play."

7. In 1583, there was convened in Constantinople the first Pan-Orthodox Council to condemn the papal calendar.

8. In 1583, Meletius Pegas addressed himself to Cardinal Julius Antonius, wherein he shows him the deficiencies of the Gregorian calendar. At the same time, he wrote the Alexandrian Tome concerning the celebration of Pascha.

9. In 1584, Patriarch Jeremy II wrote a letter to the Pope of Rome against the Latin's arbitrary *coup d'etat* concerning the calendar.

10. In 1587, the second Council condemning the calendar used in the West was held at Constantinople.

11. In 1593, the third Council condemning the new calendar was held in Constantinople.

12. In the 1670's, Dositheus, the Patriarch of Jerusalem (in his work *Concerning Unleavened Bread*, p. 539) said: "By the grace of Christ, from the time of the First Council to this present moment, the sacred Pascha is always celebrated the Sunday after the Passover of the Law, and we have never experienced any confusion which might bring us to the necessity of making some correction. This was set forth very well by the Holy Fathers and it shall eternally remain faultless. Wrongly have the contemporary astronomers of Old Rome removed ten days from the month of October.

Moreover, their new calendar provokes much confusion and many causes for disorder."

13. In 1827, Agathangelus, the Ecumenical Patriarch, refused to permit any correction of the so-called "Julian" festal calendar of the Orthodox.

14. In 1895, Patriarch Anthimus VII forbade any discussion of the question of the calendar.

15. In 1902, the Great Church of Christ rejected the mathematician Epaminondas Polydore's memorandum concerning the change of the calendar.

16. In 1903 (Feb. 28), the Russian Church issued the following opinion: "...this change, which disturbs the order that has already been established and which has been sanctified by the Church during such a great expanse of time, will indubitably bring about disturbances in the life of the Church."

17. In 1903 (June 5), the Church of Jerusalem issued the following opinion: "Any decision to change the calendar, out of preference for the Gregorian calendar, will be to the detriment of Orthodoxy."

18. In 1903 (July 14), the Church of Greece issued the following opinion: "...the Julian calendar (*hemerologion*) is bound together with the festal calendar (*heortologion*) of the Church."

19. In 1903, the Rumanian Church made the following decision: "The Sacred Synod of the Holy Autocephalous Church of Rumania is of the opinion and proposes that we abide therein where we find ourselves today. For it is impossible not to violate the prescriptions of the canons should we wish to consider some change or reform of the Julian calendar, with which the Orthodox Church has lived for so great a time. Besides this, it is not permitted to us to touch even with our finger the ancient decisions which constitute the glory of our Church."

20. In 1904 (May 12), the Ecumenical Patriarchate issued the following opinion: "It is praiseworthy and good to keep the *Paschalion* which has already been defined and ratified by the ancient practice of the Church…and it is not permitted to introduce any innovation concerning it (the calendar)…From an ecclesiastical point of view, we are in no wise obliged to change the calendar.

21. In 1919, the Church of Greece issued the following opinion: (see, Bishop Polycarp of Diaulia, ibid., p. 16): "The change of the Julian Calendar, which change does not offend dogmatic and social considerations, could be accomplished with the agreement of all the other autocephalous Orthodox Churches, and especially with the agreement of the Ecumenical Patriarch, to whom it would be necessary to entrust the initiative in such an undertaking—under the condition that the Gregorian calendar not be adopted, but that a new calendar be redacted, which would be even more exact scientifically and free from the deficiencies of the two present calendars, the Julian and the Gregorian. (It should be noted that one of the committee members who voted in favour of this position was Chrysostom Papadopoulos, then an Archimandrite and Professor of Theology at the University of Athens.)

22. In 1924, the Church of Alexandria issued the following opinion: "#28. To Gregory, Patriarch of Constantinople. After receiving the telegram of Your All-holiness, our Sacred Synod was convoked today and decided the following: We shall abide with the former synodical decisions, and we reject any addition or any change of the calendar."

We see, therefore, that since the Church—freely and deliberately throughout the ages—has rejected the Gregorian calendar, such a rejection constitutes a tradition of the Church. In order to annul this rejection, we must prove that:

1. The arguments which previous generations used against adopting the new calendar, that is,

    a.) the canon concerning the determining of Pascha would have to be changed.

    b.) it would become a means whereby the Latins could divide and proselytize the Orthodox Catholic Christians.

    c.) it would violate all previous tradition; are no longer valid.

2. The causes for the rejection of the Gregorian calendar have changed, and consequently, the Church's persistence in using the "Julian" calendar is no longer justifiable.

3. Our Fathers throughout the ages who have rejected and anathematized this fabrication of the West have erred, or, they were uneducated in the matters of astronomy, or they suffered from an unhealthy anti-Latinism and an intolerant animosity towards non-Orthodox beliefs.

4. The conscience of the Orthodox, which until the present time had accepted the hierarchy's rejection of the papal calendar, has erred.

Yet, behold how the one-time archimandrite and professor of the University of Athens, Chrysostom Papadopoulos, expresses his opinion concerning the relations of the calendar and Tradition, before he became Archbishop of Athens and was himself possessed by the demon of modernism and innovation, as well as that of pride, for, according to the Fathers, "Pride cannot tolerate that which is ancient; it loves only to innovate." "This letter of Patriarch Jeremy," says Papadopoulos, "indicates in an excellent manner the position which the Orthodox Church took straightaway against the Gregorian modification of the calendar. The Church considered it as yet another of the many innovations of Old Rome, as a universal scandal and as an arbitrary affront to the traditions of the Church. The modification of the calendar is not only a matter of astronomy, but also one pertaining to the Church, because it is related to the celebration of the Feast of Pascha. Hence, the Pope had no right to modify the calendar, thus proving that he esteems himself superior to the Ecumenical Councils. Consequently, the Orthodox Church has not been in favor of the modification of the calendar" (Chrysostom Papadopoulos, *Ecclesiastical Herald*, #143. 1918).

C. *Concerning the Possibility of Changing the Calendar.*

In order to lay a trap for us, the innovators often have recourse to the following sophistry: "Can the Church change the calendar or not?" The new calendarists most certainly are not ignorant of the fact that there are questions to which it is impossible to answer "yes" or "no." Let us suppose that we were to ask someone who has never been drunk in his whole life: "Have you stopped getting drunk?" Our friend can answer neither "yes" nor "no." If he says "yes," he admits that he has been drunk in the past; if he says "no," this indicates that he continues to get drunk. However, our friend has never been drunk and therefore, must answer us in another manner rather than by a simple "yes" or "no."

By their cunning manner of setting forth this question, they set before us a pernicious question concerning whether it is possible for the Church to change the calendar. If we reply "yes," they would declare us schismatics, since we have separated ourselves from communion with them; if we reply "no," they would call us "worshipers of times and seasons" and "worshipers of empty forms."

By this they succeed in accomplishing something else as well. By means of this perfidiously-posed question, they succeed in inflaming the zeal of the more simple among us, so that the latter might proceed to make forced and hasty decisions, untimely statements and immature dogmatisms; thus, they draw these souls away from the terrain of the unquestioning faith of the Orthodox onto the slippery pavement of scholasticism. By these means, the new calendarists have gained two things:

1. They have extracted hasty professions of faith which they utilize later to confound us, proving us to be ignorant in theological matters.
2. By means of the divergence of opinion that this creates, passions and stubborn-minded opinions flare up among the true Orthodox Christians and they become divided at the expense of the old calendar cause.

Following the example of our Saviour, we shall reply to the new calendarists with another question based on the same logic. "Can the Church change the sign of the Cross, the order of the services, the order of the fasts, the habit of the sacred clergy, the canon concerning the *Paschalia*, the liturgical texts and the other traditions? For, if the Church does this, She would not increase the number of the Persons of the Holy Trinity, nor would She refute the ever-virginity of the Lady Theotokos."

Let them apply the answer which they give us to the question of the calendar. We have never considered the festal calendar as superior to the rest of the Tradition of the Orthodox Church. When we say "Tradition" we mean the practice, expression, and life of our Church in its totality: the services, the typicons, the fasts, the iconography, the chants, the architecture, etc. and not just the festal calendar. We shall remind the new calendarists of an anecdote taken from their own journal *Ecclesiasticos Agon* (*Ecclesiastical Struggle*) concerning "the displuming of the dove." Truly, if we take a dove and displume it, we will clearly have left it intact, that is, its heart, stomach, and lungs. However, when our dove has been displumed it will die. Thus, in like manner, we can change many things in the life of the Church under the pretext that "they are not dogmas," and thus, in our legalism, we shall put Orthodoxy to death without ever having touched Her dogmas.

Most correctly, therefore, has the theologian Dionysius Batistatos said that, in these matters, it is impossible to distinguish between the primary and the secondary, because all bear the seal of the Holy Spirit. Therefore, from the moment that we ascertain that something—no matter how infinitesimal it may be—constitutes a tradition of the Church, we may not touch it irreverently and rationalistically, but rather, we say with St. John Chrysostom: "Is it a tradition? Seek no further!"

We remind the hierarchy of the State Church of Greece of the case of the Prophet Balaam in the Old Testament (Numbers, chap. 22). This man received a commandment from God that he should not curse Israel because it was blessed. Enticed, however, by all the silver offered him by Balak, the foolish prophet besought God saying, "Should I go?" whereas God had told him aforetime, "Go not." Balaam thus demonstrated his evil intent which he desired to camouflage behind a legalistic authorization from God. Yet the God of freedom answered him, "Go," in order to reveal the Prophet's "excuses in sin" (Ps. 140:4).

Thus, the new calendarists find themselves face to face with a Church, which, for many centuries, has:

> a.) deliberately and knowingly rejected the change of the calendar, through councils, *sigilliums*, anathemas and written statements.

> b.) which has proclaimed for twenty centuries that She is not an astronomical observatory, for "the Church is not concerned with the exactness of seasons."

> c.) which has considered the question of the change of the calenda "child's play," bereft of serious consideration.

> d.) which has proclaimed that questions about the details of the exactness of seasons do not concern Her, because time passes whether we measure it correctly or erroneously, whereas the Church is by grace "beyond time" and eternal in Her nature.

> e.) which has expressed Herself and taken a position on this issue and Her refusal to change has become an integral part of Tradition, admitting no further discussion.

Despite this, the new calendarists continue to ask us questions like the following: "Is this a dogmatical issue?" "Is this issue primary or secondary?" "Can the Church change the festal calendar or not?" etc., etc.

Listen well, my dear new calendarists, since all this does not suffice you, you are like the Nestorians who do not find the holy Symbol of Faith sufficient when it says "was born of the Holy Spirit and the Virgin Mary" and tempt the Orthodox by saying, "Where does the holy Symbol of Faith say that Mary is the "Theotokos?" for this expression in the Creed was not enough to satisfy them! You are also like the Latins who, despite the fact that two phrases in the holy Symbol of Faith "Who proceedeth from the Father" and "Who is worshipped with the Father and the Son" exist in the same verse, one right after the other, yet they too tempt the Orthodox by making the objection: "Where in the holy Symbol of Faith is it written that the Holy Spirit proceeds only from the Father?"—as though the Fathers who knew that the Holy Spirit is worshipped with the Father and the Son hesitated, by reason of ignorance or uncertainty, to complete the first of these two phrases! But even as there are two sides to every coin, such also will our reply to you be.

Yes, beloved, the Church can change the festal calendar, and, in fact, we shall even present you with arguments for this matter. However, they will not help you shake off either the curses of the Holy Fathers which you have laid upon your shoulders by leading the Holy Church into schism, or the inheritance of "the leprosy of Giezi" (2 Kings 6:27) and "the hang-man's rope of Judas" (Mat. 27:5) which Cyril, the Patriarch of Constantinople, bequeathed to you in 1756.

The Church can even bring heaven down to earth since She is "higher than heaven" according to St. John Chrysostom, and you ask if She "can" change calendars and monthly reckonings. We have never denied that the Church has the right and the authority to adjust the calendar of Her feasts. We simply say that in 1924, it was not the Church which made this alteration, but rather innovationists, wolves in the guise of shepherds, who according to the Apostle, "speak perverse

34

things" (Acts 20:30) and who "went forth from us but were not of us" (1 John 2:19).

Up until the 10th century, was not the feast of the Transfiguration of the Saviour celebrated forty days before Holy and Great Friday, that is, during the first week of the Great Fast? But the Holy Church made a decision concerning this, and changed the date of celebration, decreeing that the feast should be celebrated as was meet on August 6, that is, forty days before the feast of the Exaltation of the Venerable Cross—a feast which is considered by the Orthodox as a "second Holy and Great Friday." Hence, the Transfiguration became an "immovable" feast instead of a "movable" feast. Did not St. John Chrysostom repose on the 14th of September, that is, on the very day of the Exaltation of the Cross? Yet, the Holy Church decided to change his feast day to the 13th of November, so that She might celebrate his memory more festively. If the feast of the Annunciation falls on Holy and Great Friday, is it not transferred to the day of the *Holy Pascha?*[6] Or, is not the feast of St. George transferred to a day in Bright Week when *Pascha* occurs late in April? And one can find many such examples! Did the Church not change the official date of the astronomical Spring equinox by adopting a fixed date which had been agreed upon (March 21) in order not to celebrate Pascha at the same time as the Jews?

Most certainly, therefore, the Church can change the festal calendar. But since the Church is Apostolic, She acts in an Apostolic fashion. And what does the Apostle say? "All things are possible unto me, but all things are not expedient" (1 Cor. 6:12). Since the Church has judged that the adoption of the Gregorian calendar "is not expedient," She refuses to make this change. The Church has expressed Her decision by the anathemas which she pronounced, thus officially rendering the ecclesiastical calendar an integral part of Her Tradition. Therefore, insofar as the calendar is a part of the Church's Tradition, it does not change. For, the Holy Church is the Body of the immutable Son of God, Who became incarnate, Who is "the same yesterday, and today and forever" (Heb. 13:8). Even as God "cannot deny Himself"

---

6   According to the modern Greek parish usage.

(2 Tim. 2:13), so also the Holy Church of Christ "cannot deny" Herself nor Her Tradition!

Now it is our turn to ask a question of the new calendarists: "Why do you ask of the Church to change Her calendar and annul Her anathemas which Her conscience has embraced to itself and held in respect for four whole centuries?" To this very day, this "why" has remained unanswered. No real need has ever been presented. One hears only the ruminations and puerile arguments of the sacrilegious, materialistic, unorthodox spirit of the decadent West: a "monkey see, monkey do" disposition; a desire, brought about by laziness, to adapt to the demands of a world which is ever going further and further into apostasy. Let those, therefore, who are concerned first tell us "why," and then we shall see what the Church will reply and what sort of *economia* She will exercise without harming Her Tradition.

D. *The Requirements of Sacred Tradition.*

"Let him that transgresses the ecclesiastical traditions be deposed" (Canon No. 7 of the Seventh Ecumenical Council).

Of the doctrine and preaching which are preserved in the Church, some we possess derived from written doctrine, others we have received delivered to us "in secret" (*en mystyrio*) by the tradition of the Apostles; and both of these have the same validity and force as regards piety. And these no one contradicts—no one, at all events, who is even moderately versed in the institutions of the Church. For were we to attempt to reject such customs as have no written authority, on the ground that the importance they possess is small, we would unintentionally harm the Gospel in its vitals; or, rather, would make our preaching mere words and nothing more (St. Basil, *On the Holy Spirit* 27:66; also, Canon 91 of St. Basil the Great).

It should be required of all Orthodox Christians to learn this entire Canon by heart. The 92nd Canon of the same Saint confirms the above and also recalls the words of the divine Apostle: "Hold fast the traditions which ye have received, whether by word of mouth or through an epistle of ours" (2 Thes. 2:15).

In his commentary on the 31st Apostolic Canon, St. Nicodemus of the Holy Mountain speaks of the relation which exists between the Faith and Tradition: "Even as the ecclesiastical traditions have need of the Faith, so also is the Faith in need of the ecclesiastical traditions; and these two cannot be separated one from another." In this manner, the Saint shows that the Faith which is based on the traditions is neither a "worship of empty forms," nor an abstract intellectual conviction.

Behold, therefore, why we adhere to the calendar of the Fathers: not because it is "Julian," but because it has become "Ecclesiastical" and has always been the pulse of the Body of our most Holy Church. We keep this calendar because it is the one which we have received from the Fathers. The calendar of the West has been transmitted to us by no one. We keep this calendar because it was with this one that the Martyrs shed their blood, and our Fathers and Mothers in the Faith burned like living candles in their ascetical discipline. We keep this calendar of our Fathers because, according to the principle stated by St. Vincent of Lerins, it is the only one which has been used "always, everywhere, by all." We keep this calendar because, if our Fathers were not upset by its inaccuracies, why should we become upset? We keep this calendar because even if it is "erroneous, irregular, obsolete and antiquated," yet it is also patristic, orthodox, sanctified, ecclesiastical, lived and celebrated at the same time by the whole Church, both in heaven and on earth. Should I exchange the photograph of my mother which is in an old frame for a photograph of an unknown lady which is in a new gilded frame? Even if the papal calendar were "scientific, contemporary and precise" (which it is not), yet it has never given me a saint; it has never assured me that "Today the things on high celebrate with the things below."

Let the new calendarists, therefore, cease to remind us of the verse of St. Paul in his Epistle to the Galatians: "Ye observe days, and months, and times, and years" (Gal. 4:10), because this verse in no wise applies to us, for we have never been preoccupied or upset by the inaccuracies of our calendar. These questions concerning precision in the measurement of time are nothing but "child's play" to use the expression of Patriarch Jeremy II the Illustrious. Let them understand, rather, that this verse applies to them, since they prefer chronological precision to the life and Tradition of the Church, and that they, therefore, must pay the tax of their chronological hair-splitting with the money of schism.

We, however, have been taught that the time of this "deceptive age" shall be abolished whether it is measured correctly or incorrectly. What difference does it make if the date of its abolition is the 1st or the 14th of June? What will it avail us to correctly measure time, which is to be abolished, if it means that we shall go into perdition along with it? If, on the other hand, we walk in the footsteps and Traditions of the Fathers, will God deprive us of eternal blessedness for having poorly calculated the course of the stars?

We regard the Church's unity—which She possesses in Her unadulterated Tradition—above astronomical precision, as the Most Reverend Chrysostom, the former Metropolitan of Florina, points out, using the words of Tertullian: "They that preside over the Church guard the Tradition of the Apostles vigilantly; we bear witness that all observe one and the same Faith, and that they use the same laws for the government of the Church and the accomplishment of the other ecclesiastical ministrations."

St. Gregory of Nyssa says: "All men are persuaded that the customs, dogmas and traditions which have prevailed are venerable and worthy of reverence because of their antiquity." The 8th act of the Seventh Ecumenical Council proclaims the following anathema: "Let those that transgress a written or unwritten Tradition be anathema." The *Synodicon*[7] of Orthodoxy proclaims the following anathema: "To all

---

[7]   The synodical definition which is read on Orthodoxy Sunday.

things outside of the Ecclesiastical Tradition that have been introduced as innovations…or that hereafter shall be enacted anathema, anathema, anathema."

The Apostle Paul says: "Remember them that have rule over you, who have spoken unto you the word of God: whose faith emulate, considering "the end of their life." Whose faith should we therefore emulate? That of Patriarch Athenagoras, of Archbishop Hieronymus, of Archbishop Iakovos, or of Metropolitan Nikodim of Leningrad and of Pimen, the "Patriarch of Moscow?" We prefer to emulate the faith of Jeremy II, Meletius Pegas, Dositheus, Patriarch of Jerusalem, Patriarch Tikhon of Moscow, Metropolitan Anthony Khrapovitsky, Innocent of Peking, etc. (not to mention those that have been proclaimed Saints officially). Let the new calendarists who calumniate us as "schismatics," address themselves to those whom we have cited above, since these shall give an account for us.

Chapter Three

The Ecclesiastical Significance of the Calendar

It is well known that the sacred canons—under the penalty of deposition and excommunication—forbid participation in the mysteries of heretics or schismatics and even simple communal prayer with them. Orthodox Christians cannot fraternize with heretics, not only in those matters which concern sacred things, but not even, if it is possible, in the expressions of common daily life, for example:

1. St. John the Evangelist and Theologian refused to enter into the public baths where the famous heretic of antiquity Cerinthus was present.

2. The 11th Canon of the Sixth Ecumenical Council prescribes: Let no one enrolled in the sacerdotal order, or any lay man, eat the unleavened bread of the Jews, or in any way become familiar with the Jews, or call them in the case of sickness, or take any medicines from them, or even bathe with them in the public bathhouses. Should anyone attempt to do this, in case he is a clergyman, let him be deposed; if he be a layman, let him be excommunicated.

And truly, this is natural, because we cannot separate our spiritual life from our daily lives. If we did this, we would be obliged to introduce "parentheses" into our life which would "free" us of our continual remembrance of God, and hence, all our activities pertaining to our business, our family, our entertainments, and relaxation, would neither coincide, nor be directed towards the final goal of our existence: union with our God and Saviour. An Orthodox Christian conducts his everyday life in one fashion, and he that is a heathen or heretic in

41

another fashion. He has another purpose, another rationale, another horizon, another hope; in a word: he is another man. The modernists of today, however, as adherents of a love which is sentimental, have lost all notion of the close and tightly-knit relationship which exists between dogma and the administration of the Church, between the spiritual and disciplinary expression of the life of the Church as a whole as well as in the life of each one of the faithful. Thus, in a very superficial manner, with no theological basis, they attribute to the canons in question an intolerant or fanatical disposition of an ecclesiastical epoch long past. But this is not the meaning of canonical discipline. The Church is neither passionate, nor fanatical, nor misanthropic. She loves men with the love of God, "Who willeth that all men be saved, and come unto the knowledge of the truth" (2 Tim. 2:4). Let us, therefore, see what the real cause for this prohibition of communion with heretics is.

A. *The Adoption of the Faithful by Jesus Christ.*

In his Epistle to the Ephesians, the Apostle Paul teaches us that, "the God and Father of our Lord Jesus Christ…hath chosen and preordained us unto the adoption of children" and that this "adoption" takes place "by Jesus Christ," not because of our so-called "merits," but "according to the good pleasure of His will, to the praise of the glory of His grace" (Eph. 1:3-6).

Indeed, by Holy Communion in the Divine Mysteries we become "of one body" (Eph. 3:6) and of one blood with Christ. As the Apostle Paul says: "The cup of blessing which we bless, is it not the communion of the Blood of Christ? The bread which we break, is it not the communion of the Body of Christ? For we being many are one bread, and one body, for we are all partakers of that one bread" (1 Cor. 10:16-17). In another place, the Saviour Himself affirms that "whoso eateth my Flesh and drinketh my Blood, dwelleth in Me, and I in him" (John 6:56). Further, the Holy Church invites us, saying, "Partake ye of the Body of Christ, taste of the source of immortality." If, therefore, we become "of one body" and "of one blood" with Christ Himself, we are consequently all brethren among ourselves. For this reason, the Sacred Scriptures call Christ the "firstborn among many brethren" and that we are "conformed to the image of the Son" (Rom. 8:29) of God our Father.

Through our adoption by Christ, therefore, we become brethren, not according to the model of a trade-union, or some social body, or even because of our acceptance of a common ideology, but precisely on the basis of a spiritual and charismatic reality. We are brethren because we have all come from the same womb, the same matrix: the baptismal font of Christ's Catholic Church.

According to the teaching of St. Cyprian of Carthage, "whoever does not have the Church as his Mother cannot have God as his Father." Truly the assembly of the heretics—since it is not the Church—does not have a womb, i.e., a baptismal font, in order to give birth to sons and daughters for the kingdom of the Heavens. Thus, the heretic is not my brother, since he does not have the same Mother as I, and consequently, not the same Father.

If I should dare, together with a heretic, to call the God of heaven "Our Father," this would be incongruous and a lie. How could I attribute to a heretic filial and fraternal qualities which, by nature, he does not possess? If I am adopted by the Father through Jesus Christ and then return, again to the same level as the heretic, I show that I esteem as nothing the adoption which was granted me according to grace. I under-esteem this gift and I scorn and dishonor the Giver and provider, thus "proving myself ungrateful towards the Benefactor."

B. *A Clear Distinction Exists Between the Sons and the Strangers.*

Being by grace, sons of the "free woman," that is, of the Church, which is the Mother of us all, we have no right to consider ourselves the equals of the sons of Hagar, the Egyptian woman, "the slave," whose children do not inherit the Kingdom of the Heavens because, spiritually, she is barren. Moreover, we learn from the

Scriptures that the free-born sons do not have their inheritance with the sons of slaves.

It is for this, therefore, that the canons forbid communal prayer with heretics and schismatics; thus, in a simple manner, they make manifest in actual deed the sacramental reality of our adoption in Christ and the spiritual kinship that exists among the brethren who are members of the same Body. For, the heretic has neither a temple, nor an altar, nor a priesthood through which he can come to be "of the same blood" as myself, and consequently, invoke together with me my Father Who is in the heavens. Therefore, the Holy Church commands:

71st *Apostolic Canon*
If any Christian brings oil to a temple of the heathen, or to a synagogue of the Jews, during their festivals, or lights lamps for them, let him be excommunicated.

45th *Apostolic Canon*
Let any Bishop, or Presbyter, or Deacon who merely joins in prayer with heretics be excommunicated; if, on the other hand, he has permitted them to perform any service as clergymen, let him be deposed.

33rd *Canon of the Council of Laodicia*
One must not join in prayer with heretics or schismatics.

32nd *Canon of the Council of Laodicia*
One must not accept the blessings of heretics which are absurdities(*alogiae)* rather than blessings (*eulogiae*).

38th *Canon of the Council of Laodicia*
One must not accept unleavened wafers from the Jews, nor participate in their impieties.

46th Apostolic Canon

We command that any Bishop or Presbyter who has accepted any heretic's baptism or sacrifice, be deposed; for what accord hath Christ with *Belial* or what part hath a believer with an infidel?

68th Apostolic Canon

If any Bishop, or Presbyter, or Deacon receive a second ordination from anyone, let him and the one who ordained him be deposed, unless it be established that his ordination had been performed by heretics; for those who have been baptized or ordained by such persons cannot possibly be either believers or clergymen.

65th Apostolic Canon

If any clergyman or layman enter a synagogue of the Jews or of heretics to pray, let him be both deposed and excommunicated.

6th Canon of the Council of Laodicia

Concerning the necessity of not permitting heretics to come into the house of God, so long as they persist in their heresy.

9th Canon of the Council of Laodicea

Concerning the fact that those belonging to the Church must not be allowed to go visiting the cemeteries or the so-called *martyria* (i.e., shrines of martyrs) of any heretics, for the purpose of prayer or for cure; but, on the contrary, those who do so, if they be among the faithful, shall be excluded from communion for a time until they repent and confess that they erred, at which time they may be readmitted to communion.

9th Canon of St. Timothy of Alexandria

Question: Ought a clergyman to pray when Arians or other heretics are present; or does it not matter, when he himself (and not they) is making the prayer, that is to say, the Offering?

Answer: During the divine Offering (anaphora), the Deacon addresses the congregation before the kiss of peace, saying: "Those of you who are not in communion, depart hence." There ought not, therefore, to be any persons present such as those mentioned, unless they promise to repent and abandon their heresy.

C. *Distinction between the Faithful and the Unbelievers by Means of the Festal Calendar.*

In opposition to the followers of the Phanar, who have decreed that the feasts should be celebrated at the same time and on the same dates with heretics, the canons, to the contrary, forbid that the dates of our feasts voluntarily coincide with those of the heretics.

7th and 70th *Apostolic Canons*
If any Bishop, or Presbyter, or Deacon celebrate the holy day of Pascha with the Jews before the vernal equinox, let him be deposed. If any Bishop, or Presbyter, or Deacon, or anyone at all of the clergy, fasts together with the Jews, or celebrates a holiday together with them, or accepts from them holiday gifts or favors, such as unleavened wafers, or any such thing, let him be deposed from office; but if he be a layman, let him be excommunicated.

37th and 39th *Canons of the Council of Laodicia*
One must not accept holiday gifts sent by Jews or heretics, nor celebrate any holiday with them. One must not join the heathen in celebration of holidays and festivals, and share in their godlessness.

History teaches us that the Hebrews hid the date of the feast of Pascha from the Samaritans; hence, the Samaritans were obliged each year to have recourse to various contrivances in order to learn the real date. However, the Hebrews utilized various ruses to mislead the Samaritans and thus force them to celebrate their Pascha on a different date than their own. We learn, therefore, from antiquity that the people of God avoided any voluntary coincidence of the dates of their feasts with those of the heretics.

D. *Why We Have Separated From the New Calendarists.*

In view of all the aforesaid, we were obliged in 1924 to separate ourselves from the State Church of Greece because of the change of the ecclesiastical calendar, for this change:

1. undermines the dogmatical and canonical basis of the Orthodox Church and exposes the faithful of the Church to the dangerous influences of diverse heresies.

2. assails the Canon concerning the determination of the date of *Pascha*, concerning which the councils and the Fathers before us have passed judgment.

3. destroys the unity of the Church and Her synodical principles and sows the seeds of division and anarchy among the Orthodox.

4. scorns the Church's Tradition which had been respected throughout the ages; whereas the councils of the Church have ordered us: "Let the ancient customs prevail" (6th of the First Ecumenical Council); "Inasmuch as custom and ancient tradition have prevailed..." (7th of the First Ecumenical Council); "...according both to the Canons of the Holy Fathers and to ancient custom..." (8th of the Third Ecumenical Council). The councils speak in this manner concerning administrative questions which are quite inferior to that of the festal calendar.

5. does not only not represent the Catholicity of the Church, but constitutes an arbitrary and rebellious action whose purpose is the dissolution of Catholic Orthodoxy.

We separated ourselves from them because the matter of the festal calendar is a matter of piety, for which cause the 31st Apostolic Canon justifies our separation. However, an even stronger reason is that, as we have said above, the festal calendar has been utilized as the *avant-garde* of Ecumenism which, despite all the jurisprudence of the new calendarists, constitutes a heresy "recognized as such by the Councils and the Fathers," according to the 15th Canon of the First-Second Council of Constantinople.

Chapter Four

Other Consequences of this Innovation

A. *Justification of the Papal Revolt.*

In his arbitrary innovation of the new calendar, the Pope was consistent with his principles, for according to those principles he is, supposedly, "superior to the Ecumenical Councils." Yet the Scriptures teach us that "the foolishness of God is wiser than men" (1 Cor. 1:25) and that "God hath chosen the foolish things of the world" (1 Cor. 1:27) to put to shame the wise and mighty of this earth. The logic of God and the Church is superior to the logic of the world. Often, the world is not satisfied with the logic of the Church because it does not correspond to the demands of its own logic. At other times, the world considers the logic of the Church to be absurdity. The Apostle Paul, however, says that God wished to save the faithful "by the foolishness of preaching" (1 Cor. 1:21).

The first thing which our Fathers and the Councils did, therefore, was to examine to what degree the papal arguments corresponded to the logic, requirements, and interests of the Church. As for the scientific logic of this "deceptive age" which is to be abolished, it was relegated to second place. Inasmuch as the Pope has wandered away from the Catholic Church of Christ, his arguments—even if they were "logical" or scientifically exact—proved of no advantage to him. For this reason, the Church refused, rejected and anathematized the propositions of the Roman Pontiff, and judged them unprofitable and injurious to the faithful, even if scientific precision was on the side of the innovator.

Therefore, having adopted the "tradition" of the Pope's calendar, which they perfidiously mask under the appellation "the corrected Julian calendar," the new calendarists have simply confessed that they needed four centuries to understand that the Pope was right, and that our Holy Fathers suffered from an unhealthy anti-Latinism, as it were, to the degree that, despite the justice of the papal propositions, they rejected them out of perversity. Was it really worth the effort to resist the propositions of the Pope for four centuries by means of anathemas only to accept today? Aside from any spiritual consideration, this affair is wholly ridiculous and inconsistent even from the point of view of simple human dignity.

Nevertheless, Nectarius, the Patriarch of Jerusalem (*Rebuttal,* p. 214) says expressly: "We have not accepted the papal decrees, nor shall we accept them. Be they forged or falsified or genuine, for us they are null and void." Dositheus, also a Patriarch of Jerusalem, likewise points out: "Although the Pope is a heretic—in spite of the fact that he is flesh and like the grass, and that his glory is like that of the flower of the grass which falls when the grass is dried up—nonetheless, he prides himself in having surpassed the knowledge of God in fashioning and making his own times and seasons and measurements of times besides those prescribed by the Lord; and thus he propounds and establishes new reckonings and new *Paschalia* against the teaching and Testament of the Lord" (*Tome of Joy,* p. 495).

B. *The Creation of a Schism in the Church.*

Orthodox Greece did not accept the papal innovation. Three metropolitans separated themselves from the innovating hierarchy, and one of them, Chrysostom, the former Metropolitan of Florina, was sent into exile. One could write volumes on the subject of the persecutions which the true Orthodox Christians have undergone and undergo to this very day. Nuns were forcibly stripped of their monastic habits at court trials and in the diocesan headquarters of the new calendarists; priests were forcibly defrocked and shaved by policemen in the basements of the Archdiocese headquarters of Athens; churches were closed and the faithful were forced to take refuge in the forests and in caves in order to celebrate the Divine Liturgy. Accompanied by policemen, priests of the State Church entered the churches of the true Orthodox Christians and defiled the sanctuaries, overturned the holy altar tables and trampled upon the Bread of the Eucharist, the Body of the Lord! Any icons which could not be taken down were chopped away with axes so that, together with the holy chalices and other holy utensils, they could be thrown into police trucks.

Our churches were demolished or blown up with dynamite. Our bishops and priests hid themselves, running from house to house, even as our Lord said, "the foxes have holes and the birds of the air have nests" while these men had "nowhere to lay their heads" (Mat. 8:20). The monasteries were disbanded, closed, and defamed. Students of theology who followed the traditional calendar were not permitted to receive their diplomas. Marriages and baptisms performed by the clergy of the true Orthodox were not set down in State registers and thus, many children were declared illegitimate, and many widows were not permitted to receive pensions.

Yet, the attitude of the true Orthodox Christians was heroic. By the thousands, they protested, only to be cudgeled and dispersed by the police. Old men of 90 years were beaten. Nevertheless, they stood outside the locked doors of our churches, and held lighted candles as they stood on the sidewalk. And the old women, not wishing to confuse the House of the Living God with the Mount Gerizim of Innovation, would tell the police: "Close the church, my son, but whatever you do, it is here and here only that we shall come to worship the God of Truth." And truly, they did not lift up their hands to the foreign gods of the West. During the episcopacy of Archbishop Spyridon of unhappy memory, the persecutions reached their zenith. Here is an extract from the secular press (*Kathimerini*, 20/11/1952):

> Excesses! We are neither disposed to defend the old calendarists nor to condemn them! But whatever else the old calendarists may be—either naive, obstinate, or thick-headed— they are not criminals or vagrants. Nonetheless, in the offices of the Archbishop, a priest and an old monk of 80 years were treated like common criminals. They tore off their *rassa* and shaved them by

51

force. These victims visited our offices and we saw them. And we confess that, at the sight of their wretched and pitiable appearance, we were overcome by a feeling of profound compassion.

Any further comment is useless; yet how many other such facts exist which the press could not or did not wish to discover.

A similar schism has taken place in Rumania, despite the fact that the present Patriarch endeavors in vain to deny the existence of true Orthodox Christians in Rumania. Also, as we have learned, notable members of the clergy in Bulgaria have refused to follow the "diabolical innovation" (as it is called by the Abbot Philotheus Zervakos the Elder, a renowned figure among the new calendarists). It appears that the Russian Convent for Women has also refused to subscribe to this apostasy. The holy Monastery of Stavrovunion in Cyprus was disbanded because of the papal calendar. The holy Monastery of Valaam (in Finland) was likewise destroyed because of this accursed calendar. When it adopted the new calendar, the Monastery of Vatopedi on Mount Athos separated itself from the rest of the Fathers of the Holy Mountain who no longer take part in any celebrations or on the feast day of this "modernist" monastery.

There is no need to have recourse to exalted theological speculations since the Gospel says very clearly: "every tree is known by its fruit" (Luke 5:44). Let the new calendarists show us even *one* good fruit which has come from this innovation. Does it sanctify anyone ? Does it edify the faithful? Does it bring back those that have gone astray? Has it united those that were divided? To the contrary, it has brought about schisms, divisions, enfeeblement, and indifference. Do we need any other proofs that it does not come from God? But if it does not come from God, then it must by necessity have the demons as its origin, and is therefore clearly diabolical. Therefore, we sin if we espouse it.

Chrysostom Papadopoulos, the Archbishop of Athens, became a laughingstock literally. He wished to prove that the *Sigillium* of 1593 was apocryphal, a fabrication of the "monks of Mt. Athos." Yet, we have already presented that which he himself affirmed at an earlier time when he was an archimandrite and professor at the University of Athens and had written a Church History textbook. As quoted in the book *Anguish*, by the theologian M. Karamitsos, in the chapter entitled "The Profession of Faith of Archbishop Papadopoulos" (p. 39), Papadopoulos wrote:

> Still more officially, the new calendar was rejected by the Council of Constantinople convoked in 1593. The Council rejected the Gregorian calendar as an innovation which contradicted the canons and the order of the Church.

Further, he has written: "Because of this battle, Sophronius IV, the Patriarch of Jerusalem, left on a journey to collect funds in 1584. Arriving in Constantinople, he participated in that same year in the synodical commission convoked by Patriarch Jeremy II the Illustrious for the condemnation of the Gregorian calendar, whereby the Latin Church sought to lead the Orthodox astray" (from the *Church History*, p. 482 of Chrysostom Papadopoulos, as quoted in *The Executioners of Orthodoxy* by Abbess Magdalene, p. 293).

The renowned historian, Paul Carolides, in his *World History* (Vol. I, p. 253) says the following: "However, in that it was not enacted with the agreement of the ancient Patriarchal Churches of Alexandria, Antioch and Jerusalem—all of which still abided by the Julian reckoning a schism ensued." Behold, therefore, why we say that the Church did not change the calendar in 1924. If there is a schism, who are the schismatics? Moreover, we (the old calendarists that is) asked the following question to Archbishop Papadopoulos: "You say that the *sigilliums* of the 16th century which anathematized the Gregorian calendar are the fabrications of the monks of Mt. Athos. Nonetheless, the codices which are found in the monastery of Mount Sinai, the holy Russian Monastery of St. Panteleimon and elsewhere are extremely ancient. At the time when they must have been written (or forged, according to your view), Orthodoxy was undergoing no controversy concerning the "new" and the "old" calendar and thus, who would have been interested in forging such codices and why? Further, eminent historians of the 18th and 19th centuries, such as Metropolitan Philaretos Vaphides and Metropolitan Meletius confirm these documents."

Yet, the Archbishop, who had nothing to say in response, responded with police action and persecutions. Is it really possible to consider as Orthodox a calendar which brings about schism in the Church and persecution of the faithful? But if the "Gregorian" or "corrected Julian" calendar is not Orthodox, then what is it?

C. The Enfeeblement of the Greek Church.

We feel great sympathy for the "conservative Orthodox" who have followed the innovating hierarchy and with emotion we watch their battles and sufferings and their resistance against the "cataclysm of sin" which menaces us all. They themselves recognize that the new calendar is a "diabolical innovation," that it has created a "schism" and constitutes a "great mistake." Yet, they do not understand that they contradict themselves.

What does "great mistake" signify? If the calendar does not cause harm to the Church, why should it be considered a "mistake?" If the calendar has brought about no consequences—either good or bad— we cannot base ourselves solely upon a sentimental attachment to the past and thus consider it a "mistake." A "mistake" implies evil consequences or results. If, therefore, these consequences are injurious for the Church, how can I adopt them and have a "good defense before the dread judgment seat of Christ?" How can I follow something which (like the venerable Elder Philotheus Zervakos, Abbot of the new calendar Monastery of Longovarda) I consider "diabolical?"

However, not having grasped the meaning of the calendar issue, the new calendarists imagine that one day the issue shall be forgotten, and that the organism of the Church will dissolve this tumor little by little. Beloved brethren, can time alter the Tradition? Can falsehood be transformed into truth with the passage of time? God forbid! As soon as we have permitted a tiny worm to enter the fruit, no matter how small or imperceptible it is, it will not discontinue being a worm nor will it cease to grow until the fruit has become rotten. In such a case, not only does time not correct these things, but very much to the contrary, it makes them worse; look around you so that you may perceive the truth of these words.

Universal Zionism, the forerunner of the Antichrist, exercises a very subtle and penetrating propaganda in our days, using Masonry also as its right arm. In this manner, it has succeeded in removing from the liturgical books of the Latins all the texts which relate to the deicide committed by ancient Israel, on the excuse that they were anti-Semitic. By removing these passages, the Latins confess that for 2000 years, they have been suffering from an unhealthy anti-Semitism. Insomuch as they are heretics and schismatics, they have understood nothing concerning the theological issue of the Israelite deicide. Ever since 1924 you new calendarists have admitted the corruptive principle of *aggiornamento*; now how shall you react when the professors of your universities (e.g. the case of Prof. Alivizatos) support the principle of the "revision" of our liturgical texts? Truly, whether we chant such and such a troparion or kontakion is not a dogmatical question (notice, however, the suppression of the name of St. Photius the Great in the newly-published *Menaia*).

Archbishop Hieronymus of Athens favors many innovations:

a.) that the priests cut their hair and their beards and go about in civilian dress.

b.) that the use of organs and mixed choirs singing in harmony be adopted in the churches, although this is in contradiction of the Tradition of the sacred music of our Church.

c.) that Matins be suppressed, and two Liturgies be served instead "in order to facilitate the faithful." In this manner, anyone can enter in the middle of the first Liturgy and leave in the middle of the second, just like in the cinema. Hence, we adopt the practices and conceptions of the Latins.

d.) that there be a change of the Paschalia (this is still being debated furiously). The proposal here is that the date of the celebration of Pascha be fixed so that it always occurs on the second Sunday of April.

e.) that for "archeological" concerns, the iconostases in the churches be taken down.

f.) that the sacrament of Holy Baptism be changed (read "mutilated") little by little. Forget for a moment that the triple repetition of the Symbol of Faith has almost everywhere fallen into oblivion and instead of blessing the waters used for the baptism with the appropriate prayers, previously blessed holy water is simply added (as though the Fathers who prescribed that the Symbol of Faith be recited three times and that the waters be blessed directly knew nothing and we are therefore obliged to correct them). Moreover, the exorcisms are suppressed and the children are made to sit in the baptismal font and then water is poured upon their heads by the hands of the priest and thus there is *no immersion*.

Still, it is true that none of these things are "dogmatic." It is well known that Pascha was not celebrated simultaneously by all the Christians in the earliest days of Christianity, and that the priests did not have long hair. The adherents of the demolition of the iconostases might even find "archeological" arguments in their favor. But what sensible man cannot comprehend that such tactics lead to the destruction and the suicide of Orthodoxy? When we say "destruction" and "suicide" we clearly mean this in a relative sense, because Orthodoxy is not in danger and has no need of our defense since the "gates of Hades shall not prevail against Her" (Mat. 16:18).

We repeat that the Faith is not in danger, but that it is we who are in danger of falling away from It. The Faith remains the same, be it for one person, be it for a million. In the time of Noah, the true Faith was represented on earth by only eight people; on the day of Pentecost, by only about 3120 persons, and nonetheless, this was the same Faith. For this reason, we try to bear witness to the True Faith, but as to how many will acquire this Faith is a matter no longer within our competence, since it is the Saviour Who "addeth to the Church such as should be saved" (Acts 2:47).

That which is called the "conservative spirit" has the tendency to emulate the example of the Apostle Peter in the garden of Gethsemane. Just as the Apostle wished to become the "defender" of the Saviour, so do we also wish to become the so-called "defenders" of the Church. But even as the Saviour had no need of the defense of the first of the Apostles, likewise the Church has no need of our defense. If someone *could* destroy the Church, not only will we not move our little finger to hinder him but, on the contrary, we will *aid* him in his work and we shall be eternally indebted to him for having delivered us from a mirage, from a fantasy, from a human conception which has proved to be corruptible in essence, which can be destroyed, dissolved, which we had believed to be divine, God-given, incorruptible, and eternal. What a sad "Church," which instead of saving us, has waited 2000 years for us to save it!

Thus, we neither seek to "save" or "defend" the Church by our stand, neither do we seek to secure Her survival or numerical increase or to super-impose Her upon other human systems. Very simply, we seek to "liberate our souls" and transmit, as far as is possible, "that which has been committed to our trust" (1 Tim. 6:20) just as we have received it, without any alteration, corruption, addition, or subtraction. (The Latins think we are "fossilized" because of this, since they never understand anything at all.) But even if we do not do our sacred duty, the Church will not be destroyed even then; for as the elder Mordecai said to Queen Esther, "help and deliverance will come from another quarter" to the people of God (Esther 4:14). "God is able from these stones to raise up children unto Abraham'" (Mat. 3:9) or to send "more than twelve legions of angels" to preach the Gospel of His Kingdom. Yet "it is from our hands that the blood" of them that have been led astray "shall be demanded" as the Prophet says (Gen. 9:5).

Therefore, when we say "destruction" and "suicide" as regards Orthodoxy, we mean the following: Apostasy must and shall come, and as the illustrious Bishop Ignaty Brianchaninov says, if we can save our own soul, this will be sufficient, and it will not be required of us to stretch out our hands to stop the apostasy. If, however, we tolerate or endorse even the smallest deviation from Tradition, then we shall become the collaborators of Antichrist and equally accountable to God. Even though we think we are Orthodox yet we shall condemn ourselves and the millions of individuals who followed us away from the Life and the Truth. This is a crime; this is suicide.

Just as Christ had to be "betrayed," yet "woe unto that man by whom He is betrayed" (Luke 22:22); even so the apostasy must also come about, yet woe unto us if, because of frivolousness or negligence, we are responsible for its coming. In such a case we shall share the fate of Judas.

In truth, all those things which Archbishop Hieronymus favors were not dogmas in the papal-legalistic sense of the word, yet you grieve because you are convinced that piety is vilified and scorned by such actions. My conservative New Calendarist brethren, the Lord bears us witness that we love you; therefore, understand clearly that, from the moment when you tolerated the affront to piety in 1924, there was no reason why the corrosive action of this apostasy and of Antichrist should cease. In 1924, knowingly or unknowingly, you accepted and tolerated the beginning of the blasphemy against piety. The situation and your resistance has neither power nor might, since it is deprived of this action, and your conservatism not only brings no benefit but, to the contrary, lends support to the enemies of the Faith. Because of the erroneous course which you have taken, you have become weakened, and your resistance has neither power nor might, since it is deprived of consequence. Thus, you have tolerated not only the affront to piety, but to the dogmas as well (for the two are interwoven). For example:

a.) Is the so-called "lifting of the anathemas" on the part of Patriarch Athenagoras a dogmatical question or not? Can the anathemas of the Church ever be "lifted?" Even supposing that all the Latins become Orthodox, is it possible to lift the anathema of the Catholic Church of Christ against the heresy of the "*Filioque*?" Nonetheless, instead of protesting that this act was absurd and ridiculous in its very essence, your protest limited itself to the fact that Patriarch Athenagoras "lifted" the anathemas by himself, without the agreement of a Pan-Orthodox Council (as though even such a council could enact such a thing)! And now we ask you: Can a true Orthodox Council annul the anathemas of the Church? If the next "Pan-Orthodox Council" or "Eighth Ecumenical Council" ratifies the arbitrary "lifting" of the anathemas by Athenagoras, will you then be satisfied? If you will not be satisfied, then please tell us: What will you do (since you will have just founded a new ecclesiology formerly unknown to Orthodoxy)?

b.) Is the question of ecumenism dogmatical or not? Does another Church of Christ exist on this earth? Does not St. Mark of Ephesus, St. Cosmas of Aitolia, St. John of Kronstadt, and St. Nektarios of Aegina teach that the Orthodox Church constitutes the only true Church upon the earth and that those who are outside of Her are wrongly called Christians? Nevertheless, the Holy Synod of Archbishop Hieronymus, by an official telegram sent to Athenagoras, confesses itself to be a "fellow-traveler" in his activities. Why, therefore, did you not separate yourselves from Hieronymus?

c.) Is the question of permitting the Latins to participate in the Holy Mysteries a dogmatical one or not? Then why have you allowed your bishops to concelebrate with Metropolitan Nikodim of Leningrad at the Cathedral of Athens and not separated yourselves from those who concelebrated with him? You have been led astray by the protests of

Archbishop Hieronymus to Patriarch Athenagoras (which protests were expressed precisely for this purpose). And were you actually fooled by this? Is it possible to consider such credulity on your part as faith? Is it not ridiculous to make an Orthodox protest concerning the heresy of the Bolshevik church to Patriarch Athenagoras, who is the prophet and apostle of the heresy of the "common cup?" What more have the Muscovites done than that which was not already taught to them by Patriarch Athenagoras? But further than this, the Patriarch has approved of their action publicly (see chp. 5 of the present work), and your Synod addresses "protests" to him! Since you are autocephalous, why does your Church not send its protest directly to the so-called "Patriarch of Moscow" and cease all communion with him until his wrong is corrected? In the face of such deceiving tactics, can we be duped by the terminology of the protest? If such were the case, it would no longer be a question of faith, but of literature.

d.) During the Divine Liturgy which was celebrated at the Cathedral of St. Titus, Eugene, the Archbishop of Crete, placed a bishop's *panayia* on the breast of Cardinal Willebrands while the people cried "*axios*" and chanted "Christ is risen" and hymns in honor of Pope Paul and Patriarch Athenagoras. An Orthodox *panayia* was also conferred upon Cardinal Carpino by Timothy, the Metropolitan of Arcadia. Could you imagine St. Athanasius the Great conferring insignia of episcopal dignity upon the Arians? And you still acknowledge them as bishops of the Orthodox Catholic Church? Is this a dogmatical question or not? Yet, even on this occasion, you did not separate yourselves from them. Beloved "conservatives," when will you separate yourselves from them so as not to be condemned together with the heretics? Have you forgotten that, because of an illegal marriage, St. Theodore the Studite struck out the name of St. Tarasius, the Patriarch of Constantinople, from the diptychs and opposed the emperor himself? But today it is not a question of an illegal marriage, but of the Bride of Christ!

Beloved "conservatives," involuntarily you are playing the role of the deceiver. You simply are giving occasion for the apostasy to sweep over the Church a little more slowly, so that it will remain unobserved from generation to generation. This you do by accepting as "insignificant" and "unworthy of note" the various innovations presented to you. An "insignificant" fissure in the ocean floor can cause the largest transatlantic ocean liner to be swallowed up, and an amount of minerals "unworthy of note" in a drop of water can form immense stalactites. Since such tolerance exists as regards the aforementioned wrongs, the rest is but a question of time.

The "conservative" spirit can be a force only when it is permeated by an Orthodox spirit; by itself, it only constitutes a deception. The Uniate Cardinal Slipij has a white beard, and he observes the "old calendar." He spent thirteen years in concentration camps for his faith and has stood up as an implacable enemy against Latin influences on the "Byzantine rite." Does all this place him within the enclosure of the Orthodox Church?

In 1924, the modernists made soundings and measured your resistance. In this manner, they observed clearly how they could confront and subdue you. They understand that you have become weakened and now they strive to attain their goals while flattering and coddling your sensibilities. They fear neither threats, nor protests, nor outcries; all such things were foreseen in their program, and they know how to operate. There is but one thing which makes them burn; which makes them fear; which makes them gnash their teeth: *Your cutting off ties with them.* As for the rest, you are wasting your time and you are causing harm to the Church.

D. The Church's Loss of Identity.

The technocratic civilization of Antichrist strives to attain two things: a) the peas which fill the tin can have to be a certain uniform size; b) the men who dwell on earth have to become alike, like those canned peas. In order to rule, Antichrist has no need of individuals who are free and conscious, but of "atoms" which constitute cells, which in turn make up an amorphous, homogeneous, and anonymous mass. He seeks to achieve this by various means, utilizing idealistic slogans such as "Liberty," "Equality," "Brotherhood," etc., which however, have as their basic principle the destruction of the idea of the hierarchy of values. By means of Masonry, he aims at the equalization of all persons and all things. Since the family is the strength of the individual and of a conscientious society, it must be abolished slowly by degrees. By means of feminism, he aims first at the equalization of the two sexes, which would replace the hierarchal distinction between man and woman. Then he proposes a "new couple" which would possess a hierarchical "joint-rule" and equality between male and female, an equalization from the point of view of equal rights so that there would be no real head in the new family. He also institutes an equalization of vocations and the outward signs of distinction, and moreover, an equalization of external appearances; the distinction that exists in their dress and hair style must also be confounded. Unfortunately, there are few who recognize that the spirit of Antichrist brings about new formulas in the social structure which have already created dreadful spiritual consequences for the entire world. The family also is warred upon by the decay of morals. The mothers and fathers of tomorrow are often so spiritually and carnally depraved, they can only transmit to their children what they themselves possess. And yet one speaks of "liberation."

The equalization of individuals is performed principally in the religious and spiritual domain. Until recently, each heresy claimed the truth exclusively for itself. Today, however, things are presented under a completely different light. Truth becomes nothing but a relative matter and, in reality, does not exist; it is necessary to destroy the spiritual faculties which God has given man. We do not oppose the cinema and the theater and television from a spirit of pietism or puritanism, but we ascertain each day that a terrible influence is exercised by these spectacles which seek to inactivate the human mind, which itself has become exhausted and lulled and brings itself to a state of doubt and indifference towards God. Through these things, eternity has become something which is uncertain for man, and he limits his efforts to visible things which are the only things he accepts as real and certain. Thus, he joins with other men in their efforts to attain common and earthly ideals; the "things which are unseen" constitute a utopia and an uncertainty as far as he is concerned. The natural consequence of this is for man to seek to improve the conditions of his life on this earth, not in a pacific manner but a pacifistic one. The Church becomes an obstacle for him since She constantly reminds him of the futility of this world and endeavors to orient his attention towards the heavens and the things which are to come. The Church demands sacrifices, purity, effort, affliction and rejects all overestimation of earthly things. Hence, the clouded mind is no longer able to discern the absoluteness of the Truth of the Gospels, and it seeks to appease its conscience by a compromise between the demands of religion and the demands of the materialistic world. It seeks to receive an assurance of everlasting life (for itself) just in case there really does exist an eternal life after death. Antichrist has already taken this metaphysical need of man into consideration and thus, he has proposed an idealistic religion to him with high-sounding words and slogans "God is love, and therefore, we must love all men and consider them as our brothers aside from their religious beliefs." Above all else, we must "live in peace with one another with sentiments of mutual respect towards the ideas, customs, usages and traditions of others," we must "turn our attention towards always doing good and we should come to the aid of others who are in need and especially those who suffer," because "it is of little importance what one believes, just so long as he is sincere in his convictions and his motives" and many other such words does he say which, at first sight, fascinate one.

Since heresy strives by means of a half-truth to conceal the other half, there is never mention made of the Second coming of Christ, or of eternal Judgment, or of confessing the Faith "even to death;" nor are the many admonitions of the Gospel heeded, such as, "strait is the gate and narrow is the way" (Mat. 7:14); "we must through much affliction enter into the kingdom of God" (Acts 14:22); "in the world ye shall have tribulation" (John 16:33); the saved shall "come out of great tribulation" (Rev. 7:14); nor, finally, that "the whole world lieth in evil" (1 John 5:19, Gal. 1:4, Eph. 5:16), a fact which one encounters on almost every page of the Sacred Scriptures and the writings of the Fathers.

Obviously, the coming of the Antichrist is not discussed (2 Thes. 2), nor that, in the last days, "evil men and seducers shall grow worse and worse, deceiving, and being deceived" (2 Tim. 3:13), nor that "many shall be deceived" (see Mark 13:6), "if it were possible, even the elect" (Mark 13:22), nor that "in the last days, people shall more and more become egoists, covetous, boasters, proud, blasphemers, disobedient to parents, unthankful, unholy, without natural affection, false accusers, incontinent, fierce, despisers of those that are good, traitors, heady, high-minded, lovers of pleasure more than lovers of God; *having a form of godliness*, but denying the power thereof" (2 Tim. 3:2-5). Shepherds no longer remind their flocks that upon earth we are "strangers and pilgrims" (Heb. 11:13) and "hated by all men for the sake of the Name" of our Lord and Saviour Jesus Christ.

To the contrary, the world is led towards a narcotic paradise, a kind of artificial euphoria, where man endeavours to attain the maximum satisfaction possible. Religion becomes no longer a life in Christ, but is reduced to the level of a simple intellectual conviction which one adopts either out of habit, or because of one's education, or because of the influence of the environment in which one has always lived and it has become, thus, only a support of civilization and culture. Yet the Holy Church, foreseeing the degeneration of this post-Christian era in which we live, warns us through Her holy Apostles: "Be not conformed to this world" (Rom. 12:2).

Up until 1924, Orthodoxy lived Her own life in the midst of the world, a life "hid in Christ" (Col. 3:3). By the example and sanctifying intercession of our Lady the Theotokos, the holy Angels, Prophets, Apostles, righteous Fathers, Mothers, Martyrs and Confessors, the believer became conscious of his lofty and eternal destiny, that he is not like an atomic particle, or one of the little uniform peas which fill Antichrist's cans, but rather, that he is an individual, the hairs of whose head are numbered, that he holds in his hand a "white stone" (Rev. 2:17) on which his own name is written and that this name is unique. It is this unique name which gives him the property of being a man, created in the image and likeness of God, "a little lower than the angels" (Ps. 8:6) by nature, but called to become a "god according to grace" who shall surpass the angelic hosts in honor, even as the Most Holy Virgin Mary did.

He is a man because, in contrast to the other creatures of this earth, he possesses a rational soul, and since he is a rational soul and a temple of God, he has received a calling, a destiny and the possibility of the freedom of choice and of eternity. All these things make him a person who is responsible for his actions. With purpose and with a prescribed itinerary, he journeys upon the earth of his pilgrimage with the aid of a compass. He follows his own direction and is not limited to following the course and direction of other men, since he is not a molecule of an anonymous mass, nor an animal of some flock. He has received a personal calling, "he knoweth Him in whom he hath believed" (2 Tim. 1:12) and can choose his own fellow travelers.

Up until 1924, therefore, Orthodoxy lived Her own life and Her calendar was nothing other than the pulse of this life, the beating of Her heart. Since 1924, some sought to oblige Orthodoxy to follow the ways of the world and conform Herself to this age, so that Her heart would beat in time with the pulse of the world, even though "the fashion of this world passeth away" (1 Cor. 7:31) in spite of all its rationality, its mathematical and astronomical precision, and in spite of its spatial and scientific exploits.

Tomorrow, perhaps, another more scientific calendar or another measure of time will be discovered. Why, for example, maintain the weekly cycle of seven days? Why should the U.N. not find another system in which the first day of the year would always be a "Sunday," for example, with, as a result, new monthly divisions? Then would it be necessary for Orthodoxy to change Her *Paschalia*,

Her *Octoechos*, Her *Menaia*, and her entire life and Tradition once more in order to conform and adapt Herself to the new demands of a more recent epoch?

The reformers of 1924 had not yet comprehended that "heaven and earth shall pass away" (Matt. 24:35) in spite of all their chronological systems and that all questions concerning these things are "child's play" according to the words of Patriarch Jeremy II the Illustrious, and therefore, they agreed to the change forty-seven years ago. By this action, the Church, instead of sanctifying and vivifying the world and giving it new dimensions "beyond time," is obliged to adapt Herself to the molds which the world provides for Her, to conform Herself to the world and be dragged behind the world's chariot like the corpse of Hector.

A man becomes sanctified by gazing upon the holy icons and becoming himself an "icon." Consider the possibility of someone taking these icons and replacing them with ones in which the Most Holy Mother of God was painted according to the features of a courtesan of Rome during the Italian Renaissance. Would this not justify the Masonic "bibles" which declare that "man created God in his image and likeness?" So it is that men cannot grasp the beauty of Orthodox icons and prefer the flesh-worshipping paintings of the West in their stead. Likewise, not being able to perceive the spiritual and super-temporal dimensions of the Church, they prefer the "precision" of the Gregorian calendar. Hence, their icons, their music, their architecture, their calendar, their everything are in accord with their "faith," as St. John of Damascus teaches us.

E. *The Danger of Scientism.*

Having lost hope of the Second Coming of Christ, men seek the totality of their happiness in things of this earth. This "happiness" depends upon the progress of humanity; progress is dependent upon the development of science and science presupposes precision. Thus, the search for scientific precision has now become a psychosis, because the happiness they seek is purely humanistic. When men reached the moon, Archbishop Hieronymus called this "...humanity's greatest miracle." Doxologies were chanted in the Cathedral of Athens and special prayers and hymns were improvised in parish churches in honor of the astronauts. What does it matter if they are heretics when they have succeeded in walking on the moon. Behold "miracles" which are tangible indeed!

The greatest religious corporation of Greece, Ζωή, which has given spiritual birth to Archbishop Hieronymus and the greater part of the new Metropolitans (who uncanonically replaced the former ones), publishes a yearly religious calendar. Except for a bearded old man on the front page (which, apparently, is a symbol of some sort of vague deism), their calendar for the year 1970 was full of pictures of astronauts, special contraptions, lunar vehicles and the inventors of missiles. Ζωή's "religious" calendar found room for all these things, but for the sign of the Cross, for an icon of the Saviour or of Her that is "more honourable than the Cherubim"—"there was no room for them" (Luke 2:7).

The astronauts simply moved about from one place to another within the limits of nature. Our saints, however, lived like "celestial men and earthly angels" and as ones who "conquered the flesh, thereby conquering nature. And having conquered nature, they became supernatural." Yet, even if the astronauts traverse all the universe's galaxies, they can never surpass nature without possessing the "gladdening sorrow" of the Orthodox.

Are these, therefore, the things that impress Archbishop Hieronymus and his adherents? Are these the exploits which dazzle them and bring them to a state of delirium? Is this supposed to be the attitude and outlook of an Orthodox Archbishop who because of his faith and position does not "look at the things which are seen, but at the things which are not seen: for the things which are seen are temporal; but the things which are not seen are eternal" (2 Cor. 4:18)?

Behold, therefore, why the calendar change of 1924 is a proof of the spiritual decadence of the majority of those who arbitrarily claim the title "Canonical Orthodoxy."

Chapter Five

The Objections of Our Adversaries

In this, the fifth and penultimate chapter of the present memorandum, may I be pardoned, Holy Master, if I take advantage of your paternal affection by including here the arguments and objections of our adversaries. I shall try to answer them as briefly as possible on the basis of our most Holy Tradition.

A. *"The Calendar Issue is But a Minor Detail."*

From all that has been stated above, we hope it has become manifest that, insofar as the Tradition, piety, and the doctrine of the Church have been scorned because of the introduction of the Gregorian calendar, it is impossible to consider this affair as a "detail," no matter how minor one might wish to esteem it. In the spiritual domain, a commandment is not measured quantitatively, by its volume, but by the dignity of Him that commands. Obviously, the fruit of the tree in the midst of Eden was also a "detail," yet Who gave the commandment concerning it and what were the consequences of the transgression of this commandment?

1. Aaron was not permitted to weep over his sons whom God punished with death because of a "detail," that is, because they put "strange fire" upon the altar (Lev. 10:1).

2. Someone dared to collect wood on the Sabbath day and was stoned by the entire assembly of the sons of Israel (Num. 16:32-36). This was also a "detail."

3. The Lord struck down Uza with a lightning bolt for touching (a "detail") the Ark of the Covenant in order to protect it

69

(2 Sam. 6:6-8) which was the privilege of the Levites alone; on the other hand, He permitted that the Ark be captured by the Philistines, who even placed statuettes of five golden mice and five golden emerods in it (1 Sam. 6:4).

4. The holy Seven Youths of the Maccabees preferred martyrdom (4 Macc. 4-18) to eating swine's flesh (a "detail"), although this was but a temporary prescription, for the instruction of Israel.

Because of these things, our Holy Fathers have transmitted the following to us as a spiritual heritage:

1. "...Be it known unto thee that even the slightest rejection of things which have been transmitted will bring contempt upon the entire doctrine." "...Even if one alter the least part of it (religion and the Faith), one does a great act of unseemliness and immediately receives censure..." (4th and 6th Epistles of Photius the Great).

2. "All these things are truly common unto all and it is necessary before all else to guard those things which pertain to the Faith, from which, if one turns aside but a little, one sins a sin that is unto death" (Letter of St. Photius the Great to Pope Nicholas).

3. "We would prefer to shed our blood rather than add *one iota*" (St. Sabbas the Sanctified to the Emperor Anastasius).

4. "Do not speak to me of James and John, for even if one of the first angels of heaven corrupts the doctrine, let him be anathema. Now he (Paul) did not say: 'if they proclaim things which are contrary' or 'if they preach any other gospel than that which we have preached unto you' (Gal. 1:8), even if they altered anything whatever, 'let them be anathema'" (St. John Chrysostom, Commentary on Galatians).

5. "We shall in no wise permit either ourselves or anyone else to change those things set down here or to change even one word or one syllable" (Fourth Ecumenical Council).

6. "He is a heretic and is subject to the laws concerning heretics who deviates in the slightest degree from the right Faith" (George Scholarius, later Patriarch Gennadius of Constantinople).

7. "It is necessary to drive from the communion of the Church, not only those who think erroneously concerning primary matters and the essentials concerning the Mysteries, but also those who sin against secondary things; we reject these likewise as being teachers of 'evil doctrines'" (Athanasius of Paros, *Epitomy*, Ch 7).

B. *"The Julian Calendar is Not Exact."*

They tell us that, because of the inexactness of our calendar, we are in risk of eventually celebrating the feast of Christmas in the month of August! To this we answer that, in the first place, nowhere has Tradition taught us that we must celebrate the Nativity of our Saviour with a backdrop of snow and pine trees; secondly, if we were to celebrate the Nativity only during winter, how could we celebrate it at the same time as our fellow Orthodox Christians in Australia? Also, when our Church calculates the feast of Pascha, She uses the "spring equinox;" yet is the equinox of *Pascha* a *"spring* equinox" for the Orthodox Australians?

We have received from St. Basil the Great that, "It is not meet to worship seasons, but rather, the Lord." St. John Chrysostom also commands: "We do not observe days and seasons and years, but we look to abide in everything with the Church in all exactness, preferring love and peace above all else."

One must not forget that the Church has never had a scholastic and rationalistic notion concerning precision. Unencumbered by the corset of the spirit of scholasticism, the Church grants new dimensions

71

to the life of Her children. And these dimensions are incomparably vaster than the dimensions of the reality and precision of this finite world.

We encounter this attitude of the Church not only in the realms of astronomy, but also in those of history, literature and, generally, in all such realms. For instance, the historical inscription on the Cross was "Jesus of Nazareth, King of the Jews" (although this is not reported in an identical fashion by the four Evangelists). Nevertheless, in our iconography, we prefer the inscription "The King of Glory" (see 1 Cor. 2:8) or "The Scion" (Ezek. 17:22-24) because our mystical theology has precedence over historical precision. Beholding Jesus on the Cross with the eyes of piety and true knowledge, we see Him as the "King of Glory" and not as the "King of the Jews," as the historical precision of Pontius Pilate would have wished to see Him. What *precisely* is the text of the Lord's Prayer, the "Our Father?" In those Gospels which mention it, the text is not identical. Not only this, but nearly all the narrations of the Gospel are dissimilar.

However, the Church rejected every proposal to compile the four Gospels into one unified text. The Church judged that the "differences" in question do not bother Her. Just as a side note, we might say that, often, the Latins (who, by their erroneous doctrines, have fashioned a different sort of man who possesses a different logic) "lose their bearings" when disputing with the Orthodox, erring along these lines: "When it pleases you, you take a word (of Scripture) in its literal sense, and when it pleases you, you take it in its mystical sense—always just the way it suits you!" They say this because they do not understand that these words have no other signification than that which the Church attributes to them.

In the *Synaxarion*[8] of Great Friday we read the following: "The divine Fathers who have prescribed all things well...have transmitted (lit. "traditioned") unto us that we should celebrate four things..." and we ask: "Do we celebrate the feasts arbitrarily or do we celebrate them according to the Tradition?" Obviously, according to the Tradition

---

[8] The narration that describes the significance of any given feast.

since it says, "they have transmitted unto us" (transmission = tradition, i.e., in Greek, the words have the same meaning). Did they who transmitted these things do so offhandedly perhaps? No, for they are called "divine Fathers." Was their Tradition right or wrong? It says, "who have prescribed all things well." Were they aware of the astronomical discrepancies that existed? Most certainly they were. Since, therefore, they were not disturbed, why then should we be disturbed?

C. *"It Creates Difficulties in Our Contemporary Social Life."*

Up to this present day we have never known a more commercial and business-like group than the Jewish people. Wherever one looks, one can verify with his own eyes the Jewish element's role in society: in commerce, in industry, in the sciences, in the fine arts and in politics. And we ask: Have the Jews ever been disturbed over the fact that they use one calendar for their commercial transactions, and another for their religious observances? Further, are the Moslems disturbed over the fact that they use a solar civil calendar and a lunar religious calendar? To the contrary, they are quite tenacious as regards their religious life and their calendars.

Only we, the Orthodox Christians, are disturbed by the true Tradition of our Fathers and do not even give it the same honor which the members of other religions give to their false traditions. God blessed the sons of Rechab, who, according to the command of their father, lived in their tents and drank no wine, and He offered them as examples to the Israelites (Jerem. 35). Nabuthai refused to sell his vineyard to King Ahab himself in order to render due honor to his father according to the flesh (3 Kings 21), and should we lay at the Pope's feet the heritage which was transmitted to us by those who have begotten us by the grace of the Gospel, and who have marked out before us the straight path leading into heaven?

No, beloved adversaries, we do not accept the appellation which you wish to impose on us, that of "Old Calendarists," since, neither has our calendar with which our Church has lived and granted us sanctification for twenty centuries "grown old," nor have we ever adopted an older calendar than that which the Holy Orthodox Catholic Church of Jesus Christ has employed and does employ.

We are not "Old-Believers," nor are we "sentimentalists"; we do not worship days, nor are we attached to the past. We simply walk in the footsteps of our Fathers and Mothers who have begotten us in the Gospel. It would more than suffice us if we could simply attain to their stature, by the grace of Christ. With this "imprecise" calendar, St. Cosmas of Aitolia, St. Nektarios of Aegina, St. Gerasimus of Cephalonia, St. Seraphim of Sarov, St. Theoctista of Lesbos, St. Markella of Chios, St. John of Kronstadt, and all the rest became sanctified. With this erroneous calendar, they became sanctified, shed their blood for Christ and wrought signs and wonders. But which of our Fathers or Mothers have at any time committed your calendar to us? This is nothing but a papal tradition, and "we do not accept the papal institutions!" For us the Pope is neither holy, nor Orthodox, nor a member of the Catholic Church of Christ. How can we follow as our shepherd someone who is a stranger and unknown to us?

But you, on the other hand, have adopted something which is new, which you did not receive, which is not in accordance with Tradition. It is just, therefore, that you are called "New Calendarists;" you take pains to please the schismatics and heretics of the West rather than your Fathers, who have begotten you and your brothers. In this manner you continuously regurgitate worldly and materialistic excuses which are deprived of all spiritual and theological basis. You borrow the scholastic and rationalistic arguments of the West concerning "adaption to the contemporary needs of humanity," the "progress and evolution of scientific precision," but what interest is this to the Church which is more real than all other realities?

Behold, we have shown you by the Scriptures and by the Fathers why we persist in maintaining the Tradition. Give us, therefore, in return an ecclesiastical, theological and canonical argument based on the Gospel, which has constrained you to innovate. As the ancient philosophers used to say: "You will not receive anything from him that has nothing." But since you do not have even one canonical argument, you hurl yourselves upon us in a cowardly manner with violence, persecutions and calumnies.

D. *"The 'Old-Calendarists' are a Minority."*

This, of course, is not true. Eighty per cent of the Orthodox still keep the Orthodox festal calendar, which is wrongly referred to as "old," since nothing within the Church grows old. Just recently, the Bulgarian Church, under pressure from the Communist regime of Bulgaria, adopted the Papal Calendar. Clearly, the Patriarch of Bulgaria shall have to give answer for this action before God. We cannot judge the man because we do not know the conditions in which he finds himself. Yet, as a general rule, we say that the principal role of a Patriarch consists in providing a "Yes" or a "No" which he must utter, perhaps, once every three or four centuries, and which is sufficient to change the face of the world. But if his role is only one of administration, one need not be Orthodox to accomplish this. We are obliged at this point to emphasize the responsibility which the Church of Greece and, especially, Archbishop Chrysostom Papadopoulos and Patriarch Meletius Metaxakis must bear; for, by the precedent which they set, they have given occasion and grounds to the Communists to impose this pestilent microbe of modernism on the Holy Church of Bulgaria, and the faithful are left defenseless.

Fr. Theodoretus, a monk of the Holy Mountain, Athos, says most justly: "When will you comprehend that the Ministers of Foreign Affairs of the different Powers constitute the real Patriarchs, and that the heads of these churches act often as their subordinates?" Truly, if a Local Church can innovate and still remain Orthodox, why cannot the Communist government of Bulgaria demand such an outlook from its own Local Church? Soon, the same will occur throughout all Russia and no one will be able to make the slightest opposition. This is why, despite the fact that the so-called "Patriarch of Moscow" inspired us with no confidence whatever, we nonetheless agreed with his protest over the events of 1967, when the civil authorities of Greece forcefully removed the rightful Archbishop of Athens, Chrysostom (who never signed a resignation, even as a formality) and imposed upon the Greek Church the present Archbishop Hieronymus, over whose head hangs the penalty of deposition and excommunication as prescribed by the 30th Apostolic Canon.

Inasmuch as Greece is still a free state, it must resist this contrivance of the civil authorities; whereas now, to the contrary, by its silence it simply justifies the hangmen of the Kremlin and the persecutors of the Holy Russian Church; for what sort of logic permits the civil authorities of the "right" to meddle in the life of the Church and not those of the "left?" The issue, therefore, degenerates from a theological and religious level to a merely political one. For this reason, the response of the hierarchy of the Greek Church to the enslaved "Patriarch of Russia" can be summed up in more or less the following words: "You should mind your own business, because your situation is worse." This is neither Orthodox, nor just, nor fraternal.

As regards the relation between Church and State, in the Papacy we have the "Papo-Caesarist" system, and in Protestantism the "Caesaro-Papist" system, but only Orthodoxy knows the system of mutual aid, which is the only correct and theologically sound system. According to this system, the Patriarch is a citizen of the State and the Emperor is a son of the Church. One can, of course, often see abuses in the Orthodox system, yet the system itself is Orthodox and theologically sound as compared to the systems of the West, which are theologically erroneous. It is true that the Emperors or the Tsars have often exceeded the limits of their competence; yet, because the system is correct—despite many turmoils which ensued—the Church has turned these abuses into blessings (see the cases of Photius and Ignatius, Chrysostom and Arsacius).

In the 19th century, when the Greek nation regained its liberty, the great Powers imposed a Bavarian king upon it. His name was Otto and his religion was papal (hence, he was not a "son of the Church" and the system of "mutual aid" was excluded). It is true that, as a man, King Otto did his best; yet he was ignorant of the Orthodox conscience; he entrusted the writing of the Constitutional article concerning relations between the Church and State to Mauer, his Prime Minister (who also was not Orthodox). And he, in turn, found an illustrious collaborator, in the person of a Greek priest, Theocletus Pharmacides. This Pharmacides had received his education in Europe and his thought was exceedingly Protestant in nature; he was the obstinate enemy of the Ecumenical Patriarch and of Russia. Thus, in 1833, the Greek Church went into schism from the Ecumenical Patriarch (until 1850), and adopted a Constitutional charter of relations between Church and State which was modeled on the charters of the Western nations. Before this time, in accordance with the "Byzantine" principle of mutual aid, the canons of the Church constituted the laws of the State; whereas now, the laws of the State became the canons of the Church. Hence, the responsibility of the Church of Greece is great, since it has created precedents which are to the detriment of the Local Churches of the same faith, and which are now enslaved.

This is the reason why St. John Chrysostom, in his commentary on the Galatians, says the following:

> A want of zeal, therefore, in small matters is the cause of all our calamities; and because slight errors escape fitting correction, greater ones creep in. As in the body, a neglect of wounds generates fever, gangrene and death; so in the soul, slight evils overlooked open the door to graver ones. It is accounted a trivial fault that one man should neglect fasting; that another, who is established in the pure Faith, and set dissembling on account of circumstances, should surrender his bold profession of it, neither is this anything great or harmful...But if a proper rebuke had from the first been given to those who attempted slight perversions, and a deflection from the divine institutions, such a pestilence would not have been generated, nor such a winter have descended upon the Church...A slight adulteration vitiates the whole (Hom. I on the Galatians, verse 7).

We do not deceive ourselves concerning the future of Official, Universal Orthodoxy. Today they who say that we are a minority lie shamelessly, but perhaps in the near future we shall truly be a minority. Has not our most sweet Saviour warned us: "When the Son of Man cometh, shall he find faith on the earth" (Luke 18:8)? Our mission does not consist in assuring that we maintain a majority, but in guarding our Faith undefiled, pure and integral. Behold, why our fathers often remind us of the words of Scripture concerning the "little flock" and the "remnant according to the election of grace" (Rom. 11:5). Let us remember well their teachings:

> "Not the multitude shall be saved but the elect of God" (St. Basil the Great).

> "You count the myriads, but God counts the saved; you, the unnumbered particles of dust, but He, the chosen vessels" (St. Gregory the Theologian).

> "The Church is not limited by the multitude of the people, but by the Faith. The Church is there where one finds the True Faith" (Jerome).

> "Better is the just man who does the will of the Lord than a countless multitude of impious" (The Wisdom of Sirach).

> "Even if they persist in their heresy and are able to beguile the simple and the ignorant, and though they lead about a throng and assemble the multitudes, yet they are outside the sacred boundaries of the Church. On the other hand, even if very few persevere in piety and Orthodoxy, they are the Church, and the supreme authority and the protection of the ecclesiastical institutions lies with them. Even if they must suffer for piety, this will be a cause of eternal joy for them

78

and the salvation of their souls" (St. Nicephorus, Patriarch of Constantinople).

"Truth can be shut up and bound, but it cannot be vanquished; for Truth is satisfied even if its adherents are few, and it does not fear the multitude of its adversaries" (from the *Dodecabiblus*, of Dositheus of Jerusalem).

Not only do the innovators deride us because we are a "minority," but also because of our position in the Church, because of our simplicity as regards education and because of our social level. However, the Tradition of the Orthodox never takes such arguments into consideration, and nowhere is it written that one must be a bishop in order to oppose apostasy, but to the contrary:

"It is a commandment of the Lord that we not remain silent when the Faith is in danger. When, therefore, it is a question pertaining to the Faith, thou hast not the right to say: Who am I? A priest, a magistrate, a soldier, a farmer, a beggar? Do not concern thyself with any of these things. Yea! shall even the stones cry out whilst thou art silent and heedless?" (St. Theodore the Studite).

"As regards our hierarchy, if a priest or bishop behave improperly or think erroneously, he can be reproved by a simple deacon or a monk who is in order and thinks correctly; of such cases we have a multitude of examples" (St. Nicodemus of the Holy Mountain).

"It is neither just, nor lawful, nor fitting for pious men to remain silent when the laws of God are despised by those who seek to establish deception and error...nor to obey bishops who treacherously incite you to do, say and think things which are not profitable" (St. Meletius the Confessor).

79

"Take care only that your bishops are Orthodox and teach not doctrines which are contrary to the right Faith, and that they do not concelebrate with schismatics or heretics. But as for the rest, it should be ascribed to their ignorance and to the evilness of the times, or to their weak volition, and they alone shall have to give account to God for this" (Patriarch Gennadius Scholarius).

"Let the priest not err in the doctrines concerning God; as regards the rest of his affairs, thou art not his judge" (St. Anastasius of Sinai).

E. *Are We "Schismatics?"*

The innovating hierarchy has often attempted, in vain, to prove that we are schismatics and to achieve this end, they used encyclicals or…the police. Most recently, one of their most illustrious clergymen, Archimandrite Epiphanius Theodoropoulos (assisted by the Serbian Hieromonk Athanasius Gievtits, who shares his opinions) has attempted to prove that we are schismatics "theologically." His study, therefore, was written according to prototypes of Western scholasticism and thus certain people were caused to stumble by it. Even the notable publication, *Ecclesiasticos Agon* was carried away by this new "ecclesiology," invented in the midst of the twentieth century by Father Epiphanius. In an editorial, the editor of the aforementioned periodical left it to be understood that the true Orthodox Christians, unjustly called "old calendarists," are, as it were, "outside the Church."

The Archimandrite was answered by:

1. The Fathers of the Holy Mountain in a booklet published by the Sacred Convent of St. Irene Chrysobalantou.

2. Father Theodoretus, a monk of St. Anne's Skete, in two studies and a superb book entitled, *Dialogues of the Desert Concerning Ecumenism.*

3. Dr. Alexander Kalomiros of Thessalonica in a study and an extensive open letter in the journal *The Voice of Orthodoxy.*

4. Our bulletin *La Foi Transmise*, published in Geneva.

Fr. Epiphanius was literally pulverized in the theological domain; yet, he asked for this. In order to make himself heard, he was forced to have recourse to the services of judicial bailiffs in order to drag us into endless discussions. Yet, even this did not avail him.

Truly, we separated ourselves from the innovating hierarchy; firstly, because of the calendar change of 1924 where piety was flouted, and secondly, because the innovation had as its goal the heresy of ecumenism which officially became a heresy in 1964 with the so-called "lifting of the anathemas," the official joint-prayer sessions in Jerusalem, Constantinople and Rome, the official declarations of Patriarch Athenagoras and Patriarch Nicholas of Alexandria concerning the so-called "identity" of the Orthodox and the Latin Faiths, the official declaration of Archbishop Hieronymus that he and his synod were "fellow-travelers" of Athenagoras in his policies, and the official distribution of the sacraments to the Latins by the so-called "Patriarch of Moscow."

Our separation from them certainly does not constitute an innovation of the twentieth century. Even in this, we have followed the footsteps of our Fathers and we have obeyed Tradition and all the history of the Church. The deposition of St. John Chrysostom was not as grave a matter as the innovation of the calendar and Arsacius, who ascended the throne "by the grace of Eudoxia," not only preached no heresies, nor introduced any innovations, but was even a Saint and is honored as such on October 11 by the Holy Church. Yet, because he was an "adulterer bishop," many clergymen and laymen refused to accept communion from St. Arsacius: this was the "schism" of the Johnnites. St. John Chrysostom called the Johnnites "martyrs," not because they defended his own person, nor because he was bitter over the loss of his throne and its accompanying glory, but, as we read in the *Synaxarion* of the *Menaia* on January 27: "They were ready to do and to suffer all things so that they might not be partakers of the transgression of those who dared to do these things...and since they had defended the laws of the Fathers and the institutions of the Church which were disturbed, how would it not have been right to call them 'martyrs?'" And so we ask: What Council condemned St. Arsacius, and thereby justified the Johnnites for separating themselves?

St. John Chrysostom brings forth the example of St. John the Forerunner in order to show that the believer will tolerate no transgression of the laws, no matter how small it might be. "John was not murdered for having refused to offer sacrifice to the idols; he was not led to a pagan altar nor dragged before the idols; but, because of just one statement, he was beheaded, that is, for saying to Herod: 'It is not lawful for thee to have thy brother Phillip's wife'" (Mark 6:18).

What Council had condemned John Beccus when the people and the clergy broke off communion with him, and yet many even suffered martyrdom at the hands of his henchmen? Here, we bring to mind the twenty-six fathers of the Monastery of Zographou who were burned alive and the twelve fathers of Vatopedi who preferred to be strangled rather than commemorate Beccus in the diptychs.

What Council authorized St. Maximus the Confessor to cut off communion with Honorius, the Pope of Rome, Patriarch Sergius of Constantinople, Patriarch Athanasius of Antioch and Patriarch Cyrus of Alexandria when the Pope and these three other Patriarchs had been sullied by the heresy of the Monothelites?

What Council authorized the clergy, monks and laymen of Constantinople to cut off communion with Patriarch Nestorius? And yet, behold how St. Cyril of Alexandria expresses himself on their behalf: "...ever renewing in yourselves this Faith, keep yourselves undefiled and immaculate. Neither communicate with the aforementioned (Nestorius), nor accept him as a teacher if he remains a wolf instead of a shepherd...We are in communion with those among the clergy or the laymen who were excommunicated or deposed by him because of their adherence to the true Faith, who did ratify his unjust judgment; nay rather, we praise those who suffered these things and we say to them: If you are reviled for the sake of the Lord, blessed are ye because the might of the Holy Spirit rests upon you" (Mansi IV).

We could give many more examples, but this suffices to demonstrate that cutting off communion with the innovators is a result of the events of 1924 and 1964 and does not constitute a revolt, nor does it inaugurate a new ecclesiology.

What took place in 1964 confirms the fears and anxieties over the Faith of those who took up Its cause in 1924 and justifies their steps. These steps were nothing save the application of the doctrine and the example of the Holy Fathers.

"It is better it be governed by no one than be led by a wicked man" (St. Basil the Great).

"As we walk on the unerring and life-bringing path, let us pluck out the eye which scandalizes, not the physical eye but the spiritual. That is, if a bishop or priest, who are the eyes of the Church, lives a wicked manner of life and scandalizes the people, it is necessary to cast him out. For, it is better to assemble without him in the house of prayer, than to be cast along with him, like Annas and Caiaphas, into the gehenna of fire" (Migne Pat. II:1257).

"How then does Paul say, 'Obey them that have rule over you, and submit yourselves?' (Heb. 13:17). Having said above, 'whose faith follow, considering the end of their life' (ver. 7), then he said, 'Obey them that have rule over you, and submit yourselves.' What then, you say, when he is wicked should we obey? Wicked? In what sense? If indeed in regard to Faith, flee and avoid him; not only if he be a man, but even if he be an angel come down from heaven" (St. John Chrysostom. *Commentary on the Hebrews, Homily* XXXIV).

"For this reason, one must flee those who preach compromises since they teach nothing which is certain, definite and fixed, but like the hypocrites, they vacillate between both beliefs and, giving way to one, they cling to another" (St. Mark of Ephesus).

"No compromise is permitted in the things pertaining to the Faith" (St. Mark of Ephesus).

"For these sheep are not irrational but rational creatures— and we say this lest at any time a lay person should say, 'I am a sheep and not a shepherd, and I have no concern for myself; let the shepherd look to that, for he alone will be required to give an account for me.' For even as the sheep that will not follow its good shepherd is exposed to the wolves, that is, to its destruction; so also, the sheep which follows a bad shepherd is likewise exposed to unavoidable death, since his shepherd will devour him. Wherefore, take care to flee from ravaging shepherds" (*Institutions of the Apostles.* Vol. 8, ch. 19).

"It is necessary to examine and test that which the teachers say. That which is in accordance with the Scriptures, receive; but the rest reject, and turn away vigorously from those who abide in such doctrines" (St. Basil the Great, *Against Plato.* 72).

"He that dares to take away something, to remove one syllable or disturb these things in some small way at any time, be the patriarch, metropolitan, bishop, clergyman, monk or layman, or anyone whosoever, such a one is liable to the penalties laid down by the Holy Fathers and is cast out of the assembly of the faithful and rejected from the communion of the Orthodox. For, like a rotten member, he is cut off from the entirety of the Body of the Catholic and Apostolic Church of Christ" (Patriarch Dositheus of Jerusalem, *Tome of Reconciliation* 41:69).

Because Patriarch Athenagoras seeks to change the *Paschalia* completely, we remind him of the First Canon of the Council of Antioch:

"Whosoever shall presume to violate the definition of the Holy and Great Council convened in Nicea in the presence of His Piety, Emperor Constantine, most beloved of God, concerning the holy festival of the salutary *Pascha*: if they shall obstinately persist in opposing what was rightly ordained, let them be cut off from communion and cast out of the Church; this is said concerning the laity. But if any one of those who preside in the Church, whether he be bishop, presbyter or deacon, shall presume, after this decree, to exercise his own private judgment to the subversion of the people and to the disturbance of the churches, by observing *Pascha* at the same time as the Jews, the Holy Synod decrees that he shall thenceforth be an alien from the Church, as one who not only heaps sins upon himself, but who is also the cause of destruction and subversion to many; and it deposes not only such persons themselves from their ministry, but those also who after the deposition shall presume to communicate with them. And the deposed shall be deprived even of that external honour, of which the holy Canon and God's priesthood partake."

The new calendarists ask us if their sacraments are valid or invalid. Thus, according to what answer we give them, they desire to portray us as being either inconsistent and schismatics or as blind fanatics. Unfortunately, many have attempted to make premature replies, and this has provoked division among the true Orthodox Christians. However, on the day of judgment, we shall not be questioned concerning the validity of the sacraments of the new calendarists but concerning whether we have kept the Faith unaltered.

The witness of the Church for the last 2,000 years is sufficient to prove that we are Orthodox and that the responsibility for the schism does not rest on us. We do not accept scholastic and rationalistic discussions on this subject. They know the Scriptures; they know the canons and the Fathers; let them examine their own position in the light of Tradition and let them draw their own conclusions. We simply state that in 1924 the Tradition of Orthodoxy was abrogated, and we do not wish to have any relation with or responsibility for this abrogation and thus be called to account before the "dread judgment seat of Christ." As for the rest, this will be revealed by God in due time (even as He has revealed His will in other instances).

Next, they made us the following proposition: "Commemorate the innovating hierarchy of Greece and, at the same time, continue to observe the old calendar." By this illogical means, they hoped to dissolve us. But, in reality, if I could concelebrate with those who observe the papal calendar, for what reason should I cleave to the Orthodox calendar? If Tradition were flouted neither by one nor the other, then observing the Orthodox calendar would simply be a question of preference, in other words, a question of sentimentality. Neither are we "Old Believers," nor do we demand privileges, nor is the issue over *days*.

Even if the hierarchy of Greece now returned to the "old" calendar, we would certainly rejoice and would consider this as a positive step; yet, despite this, it would not be possible for us to be in communion with them. Hieronymus wrote a protest to Athenagoras over the fact that the Bolsheviks permit the dispensing of the Sacraments to the

Latins, whereas Athenagoras proclaims his "joy over this decision of the Russian Church" (See *The Hellenic Chronicle* 2/6/1970). Moreover, he told Pastor Schutz of Taize: "You are a priest. I could receive the Body and Blood of Christ from your hands." "I could make my confession to you."

Therefore, it is no longer a question of only the calendar, and if we tire you, Most Reverend Master, it is with the hope that, with the information provided in this memorandum, you will be able to report to the Holy Synod the consequences that have already resulted from the calendar innovation. Hence, should any parishes tomorrow submit requests for permission to change to the new calendar, one could provide them with facts which demonstrate the danger that menaces them.

F. *The Position of the Russian Church.*

When the arguments of Archimandrite Epiphanius Theodoropoulos collapsed like a tower made of playing cards, the Serb Hieromonk, Athanasius Gievtits, found another means to come to the aid of his defeated companion. He understood that the Synod of Metropolitan Philaret was the only consolation for true Orthodox Christians of Greece. Should he be able to succeed in sowing doubts in the consciences of the true Orthodox Christians of Greece concerning the Russian Synod's consistency in doctrinal matters, a split would result in the ranks of the true Orthodox Christians and thus, the latter would become a laughingstock in the eyes of the Greek people. With this intent, he published his first letter in the religious press in which he says the following:

"METROPOLITAN PHILARET CONCELEBRATES..."

To the Editor,

Having returned to Greece after one year's absence, and

having learned of certain unpleasant things, I judge it my duty to inform your readers of the following, which I do out of a fervent desire to help souls which have been scandalized, so that they might avoid actions which could divide the Orthodox Church. The Russian Metropolitan Philaret, who resides in America, and his Synod of the Russian Church in Exile have recently begun to avoid having communion with Archbishop Iakovos and those under him as well as with the Ecumenical Patriarch. However, *they have maintained excellent canonical relations with the clergy of the Serbian Church, in spite of the fact that the latter is in communion with the Ecumenical Patriarch.* In fact, the Synod of Philaret is in communion, not only with clergy of the Serbian Church who follow the old calendar, but also with Serb clergymen who are found outside of Serbia and who, as a result, themselves *concelebrate with Orthodox who keep the new calendar.*

To be brief, I will limit myself to telling you that I myself have concelebrated many times during the last year with clergy belonging to Philaret's Synod, and on the 15th of this last June in Paris, I concelebrated with the Archbishop of Geneva and Western Europe, Anthony, who belongs to the Synod of Philaret. *Let it be noted that the Archbishop in question knew full well that I celebrate with the new calendar, both in Greece and outside of Greece, and that I commemorate the Ecumenical Patriarch* when I serve at the Russian Institute of St. Sergius in Paris, despite all my opposition to the Patriarch's policies. Those in Greece who think that the Church of Greece is heretical because it is in communion with the Ecumenical Patriarch are obliged to think the same thing concerning the Serbian Church, which also is in communion with the Ecumenical Patriarch. But if the Serbian Church is heretical, then so is the Synod of Philaret which recognizes the clergy of the Serbian Church and concelebrates with them without hesitation; therefore, all those who are in communion with Philaret's Synod are likewise heretical..." (The italics are those of the author of the letter.)

We replied in Greek to the Serbian hieromonk, and demonstrated the perfidiousness and hypocrisy of his action. Here, we shall say simply that the true Orthodox Christians of Greece who placed their hopes in our Synod were ridiculed. Thousands of souls who are not acquainted with the state of affairs in the Diaspora, as well as the Fathers of Mt. Athos, were scandalized, not because what Gievtits wrote was inexact, but because of the manner in which he presents the matter. This is precisely what Gievtits sought under the hypocritical mask of seeking to strengthen the "peace of the Church."

When Gievtits passed through Geneva, the Most Reverend Archbishop Anthony reprimanded him for his action, and he promised to correct his error. Yet, because this man has his own ideas and designs, he composed a second letter in which he endeavors, on the one hand, to justify himself before the Russian Bishops, whom he tried to portray as being more or less indifferent to the problems which occupy us (in this present work), and on the other hand, to strengthen the chaos and the deception which his first letter had created in the hearts of faithful Greeks. For this reason, his second letter is worse than his first, because in his first letter, the true Orthodox Christians are ridiculed, but in his second letter, the supposedly ridiculous predicament in which they find themselves is strengthened and confirmed by him. Furthermore, to this very day he concelebrates with the clergy of the Synod only in order to trouble the hearts of the Fathers of the Holy Mountain.

We do not have the intention of being silent concerning the instances in which the Russian Church has used economy. Since her position is so clear, we think that no one of good faith will be scandalized thereby. But those who have evil intent will be scandalized no matter what we say or do. It is possible that not all agree with the economy which the Russian Church uses. They can, however, submit their objections in a fraternal spirit, and these objections will be examined seriously, provided that they arise from pure and honorable motives which have the good of the Church as their purpose. Any intelligent man knows that the present-day confusion by which the devil wars against the Church cannot be confronted in 24 hours. At times, we use economy in a more lenient fashion; at other times, in a more rigorous fashion, although it is always a question of the same economy. Further, any intelligent man of good intention can understand that because of the different conditions under which the two Churches (i.e., the Russian Diaspora and the true Orthodox Christians of Greece) exist, the economy practiced by the Greek Church is of one sort, while that practiced by the Russian Church in the Diaspora is of another. Moreover, the Russian Synod's recognition of the true Orthodox Christians of Greece and Her attitude towards Greek clergymen of the Diaspora who have taken refuge under Her canonical protection, have removed all doubt sown in the hearts of the faithful Greeks by Fr. Athanasius Gievtits' manner of presenting the facts. For what comparison can there be between Philaret and Hieronymus?

We must also examine whether the *partial* tolerance of the Gregorian calendar within the boundaries of the Russian Church in the Diaspora has economy or indifference as its motive. Further, we must examine if there exists a possible relation or comparison between the missionary position of the Russian Church in the Diaspora and the arbitrary action of the Greek Church in 1924. If it is a question concerning the salvation of souls and the interests of the Church, we shall practice economy not only in the issue of the calendar but also, perhaps, in matters of greater importance. The calendar does not constitute an end in itself. *The salvation of souls, however, does constitute an end in itself!* Thus, if the salvation of souls obliges us to make a certain condescension, clearly this would not be a sin. For, this condescension is not enacted with the purpose of scorning the institutions of the Church, but rather, is imposed by necessity. St. John Chrysostom says that "God praises the good intention!" However, no such necessity existed in 1924.

If someone does not agree with what I have just written concerning economy he must also condemn St. Basil the Great, who in times of necessity did not commemorate the Holy Spirit in his exclamations. But can we suspect the "Eagle of Caesarea" and the glory of all Cappadocia of being a "*pneumatomachus*" (i.e., an enemy of the Holy Spirit)? God forbid! Concerning this economy of St. Basil, St. Theodore the Studite writes that, insofar as this practice caused no "harm" in the Church, it was permissible to accept it. "We suffered no harm from this since we know also from his other words that he taught that the Holy Spirit is God (for the truth lies not merely in what is said but in what is thought); but the Church would have suffered great harm if, because of one man, the truth was persecuted…if done but for a certain time, these things are not blameworthy." Thus, our adversaries must first demonstrate to us that the economy applied to the calendar (now is not the time to speak of the other aspects of economy as practiced by the Russian Church, but the spirit in which it is applied remains the same) does not have as a goal the avoidance of a "great harm." But if the intentions of the Russian Church aim at the salvation of souls, then, even if we do not agree with the manner in which they are done, we believe, together with St. Theodore that, "these things are not blameworthy."

The difference which existed between St. Basil the Great and Macedonius as regards the issue of the Holy Spirit is the same as exists between the Russian Church in Exile and the Greek Church as regards the calendar issue. It is true, that, for missionary reasons, the Russian Church has not only practiced and continues to practice economy concerning the Western calendar, but also concerning the Western *Paschalia* and the Western Rite. We regret this, but let those who wish to be scandalized, be scandalized, and let those who wish to understand, understand.

If, for example, the Russian Church in Exile were to permit one of Her own Russian communities to exchange the Orthodox calendar for the Western calendar, this would certainly place Her on the same level as Archbishop Chrysostom Papadopoulos. But when She is confronted with communities who are, spiritually speaking, barbarians, Her duty is to draw them towards Christ and the Truth, even if she must condescend as regards the Western calendar and *Paschalia* "for a certain time."

91

Let him who is of good faith note the following well:

1. Several years ago, the Dutch Orthodox Mission sought to be placed under the canonical jurisdiction of the Archbishop of Western Europe and later Archbishop of San Francisco, John of blessed memory. The mission was granted the use of the new calendar and the Western *Paschalia* as well as the Western rite.[9]

2. The French Mission which already used the Gregorian calendar and the Western Rite asked that it also be permitted the use of the Western Paschalia like the Dutch. Yet the same Archbishop who granted the Western Paschalia to the Dutch refused it to the French.

3. Several years afterwards, the present Archbishop of Western Europe, the Most Reverent Anthony, deprived the Dutch of the Western *Paschalia*, which had formerly been permitted them.

4. The French communities under the canonical jurisdiction of the Synod (under the leadership of the most Reverend Abbot Ambrose) that is, those of Lyons and of Paris, abandoned the Gregorian calendar and adopted the Orthodox calendar.

5. Recently two Russian communities, one in Florida and the other in Pennsylvania, sought to join the Synod of Metropolitan Philaret. These communities were formerly under the so-called "Metropolia" which had permitted them to change to the Gregorian calendar. However, our Synod requested that they reject the Gregorian calendar and return to the Orthodox calendar. The communities did not accept this proposal and therefore, their request to join the Synod was also rejected.

Hence, it is evident that the Synod knows when to be lenient and when to be strict in the application of economy. Any intelligent man will understand that he finds before him a true "governing of the

---

[9] Since this study was written, the Dutch Mission, headed by Bishop Jacob, has defected to the Moscow Patriarchate.

household" (from the Greek *ecos*—" house," *nomia*—"governing"), where condescension and strictness, allowance and refusal, and permission "under certain conditions" are found simultaneously. The spiritual benefit of the faithful is the purpose of every act and everywhere ascendance in spiritual matters can be seen. But in the case of the hierarchy of Greece, descendence is to be seen. It does not matter so much at what level one is found, so much as what direction he is taking.

If one were to ask the Russian Synod in the Diaspora why She permits the partial usage of the Gregorian calendar within Her jurisdiction, She would reply: "In order to save souls, I must sometimes walk according to the 'pace of little children' like the Patriarch Jacob" (Gen. 33:14). But if one asked the same question of Chrysostom Papadopoulos and Meletius Metaxakis, what would they answer? Was the Orthodox calendar, perhaps, a hindrance to the salvation of the faithful and, therefore, it was necessary to change it? Behold, therefore, how it is possible to take true facts and present them from a wrong and distorted angle in order to give them another interpretation, according to the method of Fr. Athanasius Gievtits. Before they came under the jurisdiction of the Synod, Fr. Neketas Palassis, Fr. Panayiotes Carathanasis and Deacon Photius Touloumes were new calendarists, but now all of them follow the calendar of the Fathers. Is there any better proof that the Orthodox calendar is an expression of the spiritual life of the Synod?

Chapter Six

An Appeal to the Most Reverend Archbishop Vitaly

A nd now, Most Reverend and Holy Master, you have taken such pains to learn of the conflicts that are taking place in our conscience. In a few days, the Great Council of the hierarchs of our holy Church will be convoked in your Archdiocese, Most Reverend Master. We entreat you in the name of hundreds of thousands of faithful Orthodox Christians, not only Greeks, but also Rumanians, Russians, Bulgarians and others, to suggest to the Holy Council that, in accordance with Tradition, "following the Fathers," and in harmony with previous Orthodox Councils, it too condemn this fabrication of the West which has become the cause of so many evils and confusion.

May the Holy Synod forgive us, the true Orthodox Christians, for all that we as men—who wearing the flesh and dwelling in this world and having fallen in many things—have done, whether it be by having committed evil or by having neglected to do good, by having done something hastily, or by having spoken beyond measure, or by having turned against someone in anger. May God forgive us by the prayers of the Holy Synod and you, Most Reverend Master, and may we, on the basis of a Faith that is free of innovations, make a new beginning according to the teaching of the Fathers, for the common advance of all the true Orthodox Christians throughout the entire world. So be it. Amen.

Having my trust in Your paternal assistance and affection, I have dared to write the present memorandum, praying, despite my unworthiness, that the God of the heavens, by the intercessions of the Most Holy Mother of God, of St. Vitalius and of all the Saints may grant you, Most Reverend Master, many years in His Holy Church, in peace, safety, honor, health, length of days and rightly dividing the word of Christ's Truth.

Your Reverent Master's obedient son,

Fr. Basile Sakkas

Completed in Geneva on the 4th of August 1971, being a Wednesday, and the feast day of the Seven Youths of Ephesus:

Maximilian, Exacustodian, Jamblicus, Martinian, Dionysius, John and Antoninus.

Attention: We have cited Metropolitan Synesius with proper reservations.

Appendix I

Understanding Our Church Calendar

(Scientific and Historical Background)
by Very Rev. Boris Molchanov

The late Very Reverend Boris Molchanov composed this study of the development of the civil and Church calendars and of the *Paschalion* at the end of which study he demonstrates profoundly the indissoluble bond between the Julian Calendar and the Church Calendar. He clearly points out why a compromise between the *Paschalion* of the Holy Church and the ill-conceived Gregorian Calendar is not possible. It will not be possible to understand the calendar question without carefully studying this background material and weighing the conclusions.

Preface

In view of the absence of popular literature about the Church Calendar, one must often hear how people who are completely incompetent in this question express dissatisfaction with the "stubbornness" of our Church hierarchy which adheres to the Julian Calendar, and which does not desire to know all of its practical inconveniences—especially for our youth which is studying in non-Orthodox surroundings. Their light-minded demands for the celebrating of our holy days at the same time as the heterodox—according to the Gregorian Calendar, to our sorrow and shame, eloquently testifies to the complete lack of comprehension of what a most valuable treasure they wish to forsake. Such incorrect evaluations of our Calendar, subtly taking root in the conscience of members of our Church, can easily become great, catastrophic fractures for us.

The author considers it expedient to exert his modest attempt at a popular explanation of our Church Calendar from which follows all the importance of its preservation...As a basis for this work, the author has used the composition *The Church Chronology* by the learned astronomer A. Predtechensky of the Pulkova Observatory...All the calculations and quotations are taken from the original edition of this book.

1. THE LUNAR CALENDAR

"The melancholic luminary of our nights, which was created, in the words of the Psalmist, 'for times and seasons,' i.e., for the measuring of times, very early attracted man's attention to itself by the changes of its appearance. From time immemorial it began to serve for the measuring of periods of time which exceeded the full day. The use of the moon for this purpose was most natural and rational until man learned to make complex astronomical observations. To define the duration of time which passes between two full moons is incomparably more easy than to compute the number of days in which the sun returns again to the point of the same equinox or station. Thus, the lunar Calendar was in general use in all the ancient Eastern countries long before the birth of Christ.

Toward the beginning of the fourth century B.C., after the discovery of the 19-year cycle by the Greek astronomer Meton, the lunar calendar was already in such perfect form that it has been preserved without any changes up to the present time. The ancient Greeks adhered to the lunar year throughout their history, and the Jews adhere to it even now. As a biblical calendar according to which our Lord Jesus Christ lived, suffered for us and was resurrected, the lunar chronology entered into the Christian Church calendar from the very beginning.

The duration of the lunar month, then, was defined with great precision. In our Church calendar it is noted that: "each moon has 29 days and a half-day and a half-hour and a fifth part of an hour," i.e., 29 days, 12.7 hours or 29.52 full days. Now the length of the lunar month, with astronomical precision, is accepted as being equal to 29.530588 full days. Such an astronomical exactness has no significance for the lunar calendar, since in the tabulating not only of days, but also of hours with their thousands of fractions, it would be necessary (with any kind of calendar) to begin each new month in different hours of the full day.

"It was very natural to begin to count months alternately in 29 and 30 days. It is evident that such an alternation of lunar months is more rational than our solar ones which are subject to greater alternation—31, 30, 29 and 28 days, following one another in a completely arbitrary sequence."

The beginning of the lunar year is the new moon of the first spring month (this corresponds to March of the solar year. Since this new moon can occur on any one of the days from 1 to 29 March, the beginning of the lunar year seldom coincides with the beginning of the March solar year. The first spring month of the lunar year is called Nisan by the Jews.

The lunar year has 12 months—odd numbered ones have 30 days, even have 29 and it equals 354 days. Being shorter by eleven days than the solar year, one lunar year cannot begin immediately following the end of the preceding one. Therefore, toward the beginning of the solar year, 1 March, there always remains a short tail of the lunar year as an incomplete thirteenth moon. This does not enter into the calculation of the given lunar year.

2. THE SOLAR CALENDAR

a. The Sothic Year: Learned Egyptian priest-astronomers began to use, in addition to the lunar year, another method of chronology. Already in deep antiquity, they established the duration of time between two successive floodings of the Nile and of two advents of the vernal equinox (which they calculated at a little more than 365 full days and six hours). The Egyptians did not trouble to introduce the leap year for the correcting of the calculation, but continued to count solar years by 365 days…Thus, every four years their vernal equinox occurred one day later. Because of such an increasing retardation of the Egyptian sothic year, the most pivotal day (the one on which the star Sirius appeared for the first time in the year and on which, with mathematical precision, the Nile's flooding began) fell on various dates of various months. It returned to the date of departure only after 365 four-year periods. i.e., after 1,461 years. But this space of time consisted of only 1460 true solar years. The Egyptians solved this problem by simply ignoring the superfluously calculated year and beginning all over again, thus correcting the error.

b. The Julian Year: When the Romans conquered Egypt, they became acquainted with the Egyptian chronology which was new for them. Julius Caesar decided to introduce it, in a more precise form, in Rome. Among other things, it was necessary to correlate the solar year with the position of the sun in Europe and with the European seasons. "The year, which was adopted by Julius Caesar, upon the advice of the Alexandrian astronomer Sosogenes, equaled 365 full days and 6 hours. In order to maintain accuracy in dealing with the extra six hours, it was arranged that three years were counted by 365 days, but on the fourth year, one day was added, composed of the four six-hour fragments which had accumulated. This 'leap year' was counted in 366 days. This arrangement continues to the present."

The new Julian chronology was accepted by the Egyptians who began a new calendar with the "Actium Era," i.e., from the time of the battle of Actium at which the Romans conquered Egypt. This battle occurred in the last days of August—29 August on the Julian calendar. It would seem that it was this circumstance, amongst others, which causes our Church Calendar to be calculated according to the Roman indictions, beginning from 1 September. Therefore, our Church calendar contains within itself vestiges of all the developments in chronology from the very dawn of civilization.

3. CONCORDANCE OF THE LUNAR WITH THE SOLAR CALENDAR

a. The Lunar Year in Relation to the Sothic Year:

It was not necessary to possess a special talent of observation in order to notice that from one spring to another, from one flooding of the Nile to the other, consisted of more than 12, but less than 13 moons, i.e., lunar months. In order to equalize the calculation of lunar (shorter) years with the calculation of solar (longer) years, the Egyptians decided to count the years alternately, two by twelve months, the third by thirteen months and the next two by twelve months again, and so on. In a nineteen-year lunar period, the 8th, 11th, 14th, 17th, and 19th years were counted by 13 months. When we total the sum of days in such a 19-year lunar period and the sum of days contained in 19 years of a solar Egyptian calendar, then the sums are equal. Such an equality of days brought the beginning of the lunar year and the beginning of the solar year to the mutual order of departure, when the first month of the lunar year and the first month of the solar year began in the period of the vernal equinox. This system and the 19-year lunar cycle were made by the Greek astronomer Meton four centuries before the Christian era. (A chart of the 19-year lunar cycle is given in the original, but omitted here.)

"Thus, when the first month of a lunar year coincides with the first month of the sothic year, the coincidence will be repeated every nineteen years, serving as a visible indication of the preciseness of the calculation by lunar years."

b. The Lunar Year in Relation to the Julian Year:

Thanks to Meton, the concordance of the lunar year with the sothic (Egyptian solar) year was easily accomplished. In the 19-year lunar and solar cycles there was contained an identical number of days—6935.

101

"The adaptation of the lunar calendar to the Julian one proved more difficult. In the 19-year cycle of the Julian years there were not 6935, but 6939 full days and 18 hours…This meant that, concerning the true calculation of time, the lunar year advanced four days while the Julian Year retarded nearly five days. Thus, if in any year 1 Nisan (the first day of the lunar year) coincided with 1 March (the first month of the Julian solar year) then 19 years later, 1 Nisan would occur six hours before the beginning of 1 March."

Nevertheless, it was easily observable that such a variation was not incessant, but occurred over a very small period. Indeed, in four 19-year cycles (76 lunar years) there are counted 27,740 days, but in 76 Julian solar years there are 19 days more (as a result of the addition of one day in each leap year), i.e., 27,759 days. As a result, in 76 years, the lunar calculation advanced 19 days (i.e., the vernal equinox took place 19 days later) while the Julian calendar, by the addition of 19 days in 76 years, retarded the vernal equinox 19 days.) Therefore, in 76 years, the beginning of the lunar year coincides in precision with the beginning of the Julian one, so that the lunar phases, calculated by cycle, will occur on those very same Julian dates as they did 76 years before. In 76 solar years, there elapses in precision 76 lunar and 76 Julian years. Seventy-six years from the time when the lunar and solar Julian years begin together, they will end together and just as one cycle, so the other. The 77th year will begin not only on one and the same day, but on precisely the same hour…The result of the calculation of lunar years jointly with the Julian produces exactly the same result as if one had added four days, or better still, had added 19 days upon the completion of 76 years. So in comparison of lunar years with solar Julian ones, in the Metonic cycle, it is not necessary to take leap years into account, but merely to count all 19 years as simple, i.e., 365 days."

4. OUR CHURCH CALENDAR

In some ancient icons of the Crucifixion of the Son of God, one can see the depiction of the sun and the moon. This bespeaks the fact that both the lunar and solar calendars, with their unfailing mutual concordance, must participate in the Church's glorification of the events of our salvation. In our Church calendar which wholly responds to our divine service rubric, both the solar and the lunar calculations participate simultaneously. Certain of the Church service books contain divine services which are performed according to the solar calendar (the monthly and *festal menaeons*, for example), while in others, there are contained services which are celebrated according to the lunar calendar (the *Lenten Triodion, Pentecostarion* and the *Octoechos*).

We reckon according to the lunar calendar our most important feast day, the Resurrection of Christ, as well as all the holy days closely bound to it in content and dependent upon it according to chronology (the Great Lent with the preparatory weeks, Ascension of the Lord, the beginning of Peter's Fast and its duration, and the whole calculation of Pentecost).

Since the beginning of the lunar year (1 Nisan) seldom coincided with the beginning of the solar Julian year (1 March), the feast of the Christian *Pascha* occurs on various dates of the Julian months of March and April. The calculations of the time of *Pascha* according to lunar and solar chronology became a complex science called the *Paschalion*. In this area of precise and indissoluble lunar concordance with Julian chronology, we have the unsurpassed work of the Alexandrian astronomers (end of the 3rd century) which the Church carefully preserves, and which is printed in some divine service books in the form of the *Paschal* Almanac.

5. THE UNILATERAL BOND OF THE LUNAR CALENDAR WITH THE JULIAN IN THE ORTHODOX CHRISTIAN PASCHALION

Having studied our *Paschalion*, we are irresistibly penetrated with awe at the ingenious work of the Alexandrian scientists who attained, in the *Paschalion*, an unalterable bond of the lunar with the solar Julian calendar. Alexandrian astronomers of the third century, knew well the retardation of the Julian calendar from the sun. Nevertheless, they did not reject the Julian calendar, but wisely made use of its errors for a stable concordance with the lunar year, which lies at the basis of our *Paschalion*. The Julian calendar remains behind the true solar time, and the lunar one also remains behind together with the Julian calendar. "The lunar year is found to be eternally tied to the Julian one and a perpetual retardation of the former from the latter is not possible. The lag of the Julian year is equal to the lag of the lunar one. The equinox retards equally in both chronologies."

The difference between the lunar and our Julian calendar does not exceed an hour and a half in the lapse of a thousand years. We can see for ourselves how all the *Paschal* full-moons calculated for thousands of years ahead in our *Paschalion* fall precisely on all the indicated dates of the Julian calendar, but do not at all coincide with the Gregorian calendar.

The unalterable tie of the lunar calendar with the Julian is made especially vivid by the following constant, periodical phenomena: we know that the lunar cycle equals 19 years while the solar cycle equals 28 years. Let us analyze these numbers by primary multipliers: 19=1x19; 28=4x7. What happens when we cross-multiply them? 19x4=76, i.e., that period of 76 years upon whose lapse the beginning of the lunar year coincides in precision with the beginning of the Julian one (as shown in chapter three).

Now, if we multiply 76 by 7, we arrive at 532, i.e., that period upon whose lapse, *Pascha* again occurs on the same days and months on which it was celebrated from the very beginning and during the whole length of the indiction.

In view of such a stable bond of the lunar year with the Julian, there can be no talk of any change from the Julian calendar, for otherwise there would unavoidably occur a violation of the entire well-formed and harmonious system of our *Paschalion* and the introduction of a great confusion in all *Paschal* calculations.

Sorrowfully, the light-minded experiment of changing the Julian calendar was made in Rome and now one can see its pitiful consequences. (It has made obedience to the holy canons, given to the Holy Church by the Holy Spirit, impossible for Rome, which was forced, by the new calendar to abandon the canonical *Paschalion*).

6. THE LATIN REFORM OF THE CALENDAR AND ITS CONSEQUENCES UPON LITURGICAL HARMONY

In the Vatican, in the tower of the four winds, there is a room which has preserved the name *Sala del Calendaris*—the Hall of the Calendar. In 1582, Pope Gregory XIII sat in this hall and observed with interest the sun's ray which passed along the floor on which was drawn a line from north to south. At that time the Italian scientists Ignatius Dante, Aloysius Lilius, Christopher Clavius and Pietro Cicchone, convinced the Pope that the calendar falls behind the sun and is in need of correction. The Pope demanded proof. Then the scientists drew a line on the floor of the Hall of the Calendar, pierced the south wall for the entry into the room of the sun's rays. The Pope was invited to become visually convinced of the correctness of their assertions.

They proved to be right: the days of the solstices and equinoxes were removed by ten full days. The sun itself testified to the retardation of the Julian calendar. The Pope was convinced. In 1582, the reform of the calendar was passed. After October 4, it at once became October 15. If, however, the knowledge of the Italian scientists of the 16th century had even approached the knowledge of the compilers of the *Paschalion* (the Alexandrian scientists of the 3rd century), then they themselves would have rejected their own plan of calendar reform. Unfortunately, they were far from the enlightenment of the Alexandrian scientists who already, in the 3rd century knew very well what the Italian scientists came to understand only in the 16th century—the retardation of the calendar.

The reform itself was instituted primitively and coarsely. For, instead of ordering that October 5 would be, instead, October 15, the reform could have been introduced gradually and orderly over a forty-year span simply by not counting the leap year days, but considering

105

all years to be plain for that forty-year period. It would seem, in fact, that, thanks to such a primitive method of reform, the first violators of it were the reformers themselves, namely, the Italian astronomers who were at once met with various practical difficulties. How could they maintain the journal of their astronomical observations in which they had to note not only the days, but the hours and minutes, having created a gap of ten full days? How could they make their calculations after, by means of their reform, they had broken off all bonds with the uniformity of the former calendar? The only way out of this quandary would have been a return to the Julian calendar and a continued use of it in all calculations with a very simple change of the results of their calculations obtained in the dates of the Julian calendar by new ciphers (i.e., the same accuracy of chronology would have been obtained, and unity of the solar and lunar chronology would not have been broken).

Was it worth making a reform of the calendar because of the retardation in the Julian chronology? The most decisive opponent to the Latin reform turned out to be the lunar chronology which could not possibly have any unity with the new calendar. Thus, the Italian reformers were forced to change it and the whole *Paschalion*. The most beautiful work of the Alexandrian scientists was mutilated and distorted. Their ingeniously simple and precise system was replaced by a new and cumbersome system—one neither directed toward, nor attaining, the exalted aim of the former. The harmony of the lunar year with the solar one was violated. "The order of calculation of lunar cycles was changed, and the reformers began to calculate the movements of the moon artificially by the introduction of an acceleration by one full day in 310 years. The result was that their *Pascha*, in some years, coincides with the Jewish Passover—an event which is specifically condemned and forbidden by the First Ecumenical Council...If the overly self-confident compilers of the new calendar, Aloysius Lilius and his colleagues, had troubled themselves to study the Jewish calendar contemporary with them, they would not have introduced the unfortunate lunar alteration."

The replacing of the Julian calendar by the Gregorian was like replacing a highly artistic creation by a crude, poorly executed wood cut. The Italian scientists of the 16th century, with their new calendar, erected a monument to their own personal, self-confident ignorance.

7. IS COMPROMISE POSSIBLE?

The Latin reformers, as we have seen, having changed the solar calendar, were forced to alter the lunar chronology as well, and, together with the lunar year, to change the entire *Paschalion.*

Many Orthodox Christians, while understanding the complete impossibility for the Holy Church to reject the lunar calendar and the canonical rules for celebrating *Pascha,* do not realize the indissoluble bond of our *Paschalion* with the Julian calendar. Such misinformed people often speak about a compromise proposal: to leave our *Paschalion* unchanged, i.e., to celebrate *Pascha* and all feasts and days bound with it, according to the lunar calendar; but to perform Divine Services according to the new Gregorian calendar. Such a proposal is strengthened by notions about the necessity for our school children who must study in non-Orthodox Christian schools, to celebrate all holy days according to the legal vacations of the non-Orthodox, on the Gregorian reckoning. They do not wish the inconvenience of celebrating the holy days according to the calendar of the Holy Church, which is not used by the secular authorities here. We will not argue about some of the difficulties which our school children face in keeping the Orthodox Christian holy days according to our Church calendar. Such difficulties are encountered, of course, but it is necessary not to exaggerate them. Jewish and Mohammedan children find it possible to observe their feast days without changing their calendar. (If even non-Christians have the courage and depth of devotion to maintain their fasts when others are feasting and to maintain faithfully their holy day chronology, what excuse could we possibly have for doing less?) Why is it that only amongst us there arise such desires to surrender our Julian calendar?

Looking at the wonderful accord of the lunar with the Julian calendar, it can be seen that it is completely impossible to change the latter without altering the former. The sad experience of the Latin reform of the solar calendar, which reform could not avoid altering (artificially) the lunar year, must be a constant warning for us.

Authors of compromising proposals cannot discount the completely unallowable situations which inevitably arise from attempts to use the canonical *Paschalion* in conjunction with the Gregorian calendar. An example of such a situation occurred in 1959. In that year, *Pascha* was on April 20. Trinity Day fell on June 8 (all dates of the lunar year are indicated according to the dates of the Julian calendar). Eight days later, on June 16, the fast of St. Peter began and continued to the day of the Holy Chief-Apostles, Peter and Paul (June 29). If the Gregorian (new) calendar was used, the beginning of Peter's fast would have fallen on June 29, the very day of the feast of Sts. Peter and Paul and so Peter's fast would not have been observed at all. This would occur in all cases when *Pascha* falls from April 20 to 25 (OS). Peter's fast would disappear under the Gregorian (new) calendar.

The Holy Church can in no way renounce the apostolic ordinances. Consequently, it cannot accept the Gregorian (new) calendar, even under compromise conditions.

Appendix II

The Appearance of the Sign of the Cross of Our Lord Jesus Christ Near Athens in 1925 – Commemorated on 14 (27) September

In the early 1900's, and especially in the 1920's, there were strong anti-Church and secularist forces in power in Greece and in the Ecumenical Patriarchate. Among the actions of these forces, there was introduced, by force, the Gregorian calendar. The Gregorian calendar is adequate for the functions of business, the stock exchange, and other worldly, secular activities. Liturgically, however, it is practically useless, even harmful. It is in no way possible to reconcile the Gregorian calendar with our canonical, Orthodox Christian *Paschalion.* Moreover, the introduction of a Church calendar change by a local church created an unacceptable liturgical disunity within the Church Itself.

Vast numbers of the people of Greece refused to accept these anti-canonical, anti-Church changes being forced upon them by state police power. Such people suffered, and continue to suffer persecution, imprisonment, and deprivation at the hands of secular police powers. But the spiritual eyes of true Orthodox Christians saw clearly even if, at the time, they did not completely comprehend the evil of the new calendar. It was a forerunner and a sign of the greatest heresy in the history of the world—Ecumenism. Many people, however, became confused. Some began to waver. Just as the Arians were in control of the worldly power in 351 and were able to force their heresy upon the empire, so now, the calendar renovationists controlled the worldly power of Greece. In such a troubled and dangerous time, the All-Merciful God heeded the needs of His people. Again, as in 351, God sent a wondrous apparition of the sign of the All-Honourable Cross to seal the truth and put the false teachers to shame.

The appearance of the sign of the Cross took place in this manner:

In 1925, on the eve of the feast of the Exaltation of the Honourable and Life-giving Cross of our Saviour, September 14 according to the Orthodox Church calendar, the all-night vigil was served at the church of St. John the Theologian in suburban Athens. By 9 o'clock that evening, more than 2,000 of the true-Orthodox faithful had gathered in and around the church for the service, since very few true-Orthodox churches had been accidentally left open by the civil authorities. Such a large gathering of people could not, however, go unnoticed by the authorities. Around eleven PM the authorities dispatched a battalion of police to the church "to prevent any disorders which might arise from such a large gathering." The gathering was too large for the police to take any direct action or to arrest the priest at that time, and so they mingled with the crowd of worshipers in the already overflowing courtyard of the church.

Then, regardless of the true motives for their presence, against their own will, but according to the Will which exceeds all human power, they became participants in the miraculous experience of the crowd of believers.

At eleven thirty PM, there began to appear in the heavens above the church, in the direction of North-East, a bright, radiant Cross of light. The light not only illuminated the church and the faithful but, in its rays, the stars of the clear, cloudless sky became dim and the church-yard was filled with an almost tangible light. The form of the Cross itself was an especially dense light and it could be clearly seen as a Byzantine cross with an angular cross bar toward the bottom. This heavenly miracle lasted for half an hour, until midnight, and then the Cross began slowly to raise up vertically, as the cross in the hands of the priest does in the ceremony of the Elevation of the Cross in church. Having come straight up, the Cross began gradually to fade away.

110

The human language is not adequate to convey what took place during the apparition. The entire crowd fell prostrate upon the ground with tears and began to sing hymns praising the Lord with one heart and one mouth. The police were among those who wept, suddenly discovering, in the depths of their hearts, a childlike faith. The crowd of believers and the battalion of police were transformed into one, unified flock of faithful. All were seized with a holy ecstasy. The vigil continued until four am, when all this human torrent streamed back into the city, carrying the news of the miracle because of which they were still trembling and weeping.

Many of the unbelievers, sophists and renovationists, realizing their sin and guilt, but unwilling to repent, tried by every means to explain away or deny this miracle. The fact that the form of the cross had been so sharply and clearly that of the Byzantine (sometimes called the Russian) Cross, with three cross-bars, the bottom one at an angle, completely negated any arguments of accidental physical phenomenon.

The fact that such an apparition of the Cross had also occurred during the height of the first great heresy must strike the Orthodox with an especial sense of the magnitude of the importance of the calendar question and of all that is connected with it. No sensible person can discuss this issue lightly, with secular reasoning or with worldly arguments. Renovationists, like the Arians in 351, are left without extenuation or mitigation.

TROPARION Tone 3

When the storm of Ecumenism began to rage, O Saviour, against Thy Holy Church, and the faithful were tempest-tossed as were the Apostles on the Sea of Galilee, Thou didst vouchsafe to seal with the sign of Thine all-Honourable Cross, O Merciful One, the calendar of Thy Church as a symbol of the true way. Wherefore, we cry with joy: Through the prayers of the Theotokos, O Saviour, save us.

KONTAKION Pl. of the 4th Tone

Athens rejoiced, O Saviour, to behold the wonder of Thy compassion; for Thou didst cause the symbol of our salvation to shine forth for the consolation of the faithful and for the testimony of the truth. Wherefore, O Holy One, we faithful magnify Thine ineffable condescension.

Appendix III

The Sigillion of 1583 Against The Calendar Innovation of the Latins: Myth or Reality?

Introduction

Since the original publication of *The Calendar Question* by Father Basile Sakkas in 1973, new scholarship has brought to light that one of the documents that is regularly used to prove that the new calendar innovation has been condemned in a conciliar fashion, the so-called Sigillion of 1583, is not authentic. What was believed then to be a legitimate document condemning the new calendar has since been proven through patristic scholarship to be a historical forgery by a singular monk on Mount Athos. In this debate, two camps have come to the forefront. The first is those who believe that three separate Church councils have in their finality condemned and anathematized believers who have accepted the Gregorian Calendar (New Calendar). The second being those that accept this ecumenical innovation and violation of Holy Tradition as valid, dismissing the Orthodox disapprobation of the new calendar as a myth or something based entirely on forged documents.

However, despite this one historical document being referenced in the original volume by Fr. Basile and subsequently being proven to be a historical forgery by an unscrupulous Athonite monk, thirty-eight years after its original publication, the remainder of his book with the arguments contained therein, prove on their own merit that the new calendar is an innovation, the first step into heretical ecumenism, and a rejection of Orthodox Church tradition.

The former acting president of the former Holy Synod in Resistance (SiR), Bishop Cyprian of Oropos who, as a remarkable patristic scholar, discusses these two camps with academic

113

precision; on one hand exposing the misinterpretations that have arisen on account of certain documents condemning the new calendar that are, in fact, unreliable and forgeries, and on the other hand, exposing the rejection of legitimate historical records for self-serving claims that the new calendar innovation has never in actuality been officially condemned by the Holy Orthodox Church.

This patristic study produced by Bishop Cyprian of Oropos is of a singular importance in that it demonstrates how both those on the extreme left and right with regard to the calendar question are misguided and misinformed in many aspects concerning the new calendar innovation. Both parties have unfortunately based their varying opinions on false presuppositions, a lack of historically factual information, and faulty assessments of the historical record. It is our intention to present this work by Bishop Cyprian to help dispel the accusation that the inclusion of the forged Sigillion of 1583 into this original work by Father Basile Sakkas does not take away the primary thesis of the book that the new calendar is, in fact, an innovation, has been condemned in various other ways by the Orthodox Church, and should be rejected by those faithful to the traditions of the Orthodox Church.

Excerpt from "The Sigillion of 1583 Against The Calendar Innovation of the Latins: Myth or Reality?" [10]

By Metropolitan Cyprian II of Oropos & Phyle

The Athonite Transcriptions of Monk Iakovos

1. In 1858, an Athonite monk, Father Iakovos of New Skete, transcribed various documents, from among the aforementioned, concerning the repudiation and condemnation of the Gregorian Calendar, which are to be found in Codex No. 258 of the library of Kavsokalyvia. It was from this codex that Codex No. 722 of the Monastery of St. Panteleimon was compiled.

2. The original texts compiled by Father Iakovos and the items deriving from him in these codices constitute a patently arbitrary admixture of disparate documents of different dates, into which, moreover, alterations and additions have also been introduced, to the point that one wonders what ultimately was the intention of Father Iakovos, who doctored, distorted, and falsified them.

3. This truly deplorable farrago put together by Father Iakovos, which is fancifully characterized as a "Patriarchal and Synodal *Sigillion*" "accompanied by sanctions and anathemas," has been used in self-serving ways since 1924, and has appeared in many versions,13 each worse than the other. The form of it that has finally prevailed bears a title unattested in the original texts from the sixteenth and seventeenth centuries: *"Sigillion* of the Patriarchal formulation of an

---

10   This is an excerpt from the above-named article which is an entire treatment of the so-called Sigillion of 1583 in which modern scholarship has proven to be a historical forgery, yet does not affect the primary thesis and overall argument of this published work by Father Basile Sakkas. "The Sigillion of 1583 Against the Calendar Innovation of the Latins: Myth or Reality," The Orthodox Archive, accessed January 7, 2024, https://www.theorthodoxarchive.org/file-share/7f1cfe7a-7d90-471c-944d-1c00b2b2915c

Encyclical to Orthodox Christians throughout the world not to accept the modernistic *Paschalion* or calendar of the innovated *Menologion*, but to abide by what was well formulated once and for all by the three hundred and eighteen (318) Holy God-bearing Fathers of the Holy First Ecumenical Synod, under pain of sanction and anathema."

4. In the aforementioned Athonite codices the following three texts, which have no relation to each other and in which, as we have said, alterations and additions have been introduced, were mixed and spliced together:

a. The joint Epistle of Patriarchs Jeremiah and Sylvester to the Armenians, dated November 20, 1583;

b. The "Synodal Act" of 1593;

c. The *Tomos* of Cyril Loukaris (1570-1638), Patriarch of Alexandria, issued in Targoviste, Moldo-Wallachia, in 1616.

5. In the predominant version of the *Sigillion* there are five blatant alterations and additions arbitrarily imported by the compiler.

a. The title: a pure invention of the compiler.

b. The date: this document was allegedly composed on November 20, 1583, which is actually the date of the joint Epistle of Patriarchs Jeremiah and Sylvester, whereas the text presented in the *Sigillion* was composed in 1616.

c. The signatures: Patriarchs Jeremiah (†1595) and Sylvester (†1590) were no longer alive in 1616, and Patriarch Sophronios had already abdicated by 1608.

116

d. The text: it belongs to Loukaris (1616) and not to the Synod of 1583, and its content is not only entirely unrelated to the calendar question, but is also appallingly garbled.

e. The anathema: whereas in Loukaris' text, there are six anathemas, pertaining to Roman Catholic teachings, the compiler has added to the *Sigillion* a seventh anathema concerning all who follow the "newly invented *Paschalion* and the New *Menologion* of the atheist astronomers of the Pope [*sic*]."

6. The argument that the content of the two aforementioned Athonite codices is supposedly—confirmed by a manuscript codex from Sinai, from which the *Sigillion* was published in Romania by Archimandrite Porfiry Ouspensky, who visited Sinai in 1850, is without foundation, since, on the basis of our Romanian sources, it is evident that Father Porfiry published in translation only the "Alexandrian *Tomos*" of Meletios Pegas and his epistle to Tsar Fyodor Ivanovich of Russia, dated September 12, 1594.

Fruitless Conflict

1. In the wake of the calendar innovation in 1924—the first step towards implementing the plan for rapprochement between divided Christians, in conformity with the ecumenist 1920 Encyclical of the Patriarchate of Constantinople—the so-called *Sigillion* of 1583 has proved to be a "rock of offense" between ecumenists and anti-ecumenists, between innovators and anti-innovationists, who expend their energies in a fruitless conflict, thereby willy-nilly shifting attention to an almost insignificant issue.

2. The putative *Sigillion* of 1583 essentially has nothing to offer to the sacred cause of resistance against the ecclesiological heresy of ecumenism. Indeed, even if it were genuine, it would not take effect automatically and instantaneously, expelling the innovators from the

Church forthwith, since an anathema, in order to take effect, requires a special Synodal judgment on the basis of Orthodox Church order.

3. One way or another, Orthodox resistance and walling-off do not depend on the contrived *Sigillion* of 1583, nor even on the Synodal decisions of the sixteenth century, for, although these deserve our respect and give us guidance, they do not pertain directly to the contemporary form of the calendar question: in 1924, the innovation of Pope Gregory XIII was partially implemented, while the Orthodox *Paschalion* remained intact.

4. This partial acceptance of the Gregorian Calendar demands a new and specific assessment of the issue by a Pan-Orthodox Synod, as the Confessor-Hierarch Metropolitan Chrysostomos of Phlorina (†1955) very astutely maintained. He very severely condemned the view that, supposedly, "it is unnecessary and superfluous to convene a Pan–Orthodox Synod or a major local Synod for the authoritative and definitive condemnation of the calendar innovation...since the Pan–Orthodox Synods of 1583, 1587, and 1593 condemned the Gregorian Calendar"; the innovation of 1924, which applied "the Gregorian Calendar only to the fixed Feasts and not to Pascha, which was the main reason why the Gregorian Calendar was condemned as conflicting with the Seventh Apostolic Canon, is an issue that appears for the first time in the history of the Orthodox Church. Consequently, the convocation of a Pan–Orthodox Synod is not only not superfluous... but is actually required for the canonical and authoritative adjudication of this issue."

Bishop Cyprian of Oropos,
Acting President

Phyle, Attica
May 13, 2011 (Old Style)
Holy Martyr Glykeria

Bibliography

Greek Sources:

The Agony in the Garden of Gethsemane, by Stavros Karamit so-Gambrulias; Athens, 1961.

Dialogues of the Desert Concerning Ecumenism, by Theodoretus a Monk of the Holy Mountain; Athens, 1971.

The Executioners of Orthodoxy in 1924, by Magdalene, Abbess of the Convent of the Ascension in Kozani; Athens, 1970.

The Apology of an Orthodox Christian, by George Antonopoulos.

Memorandum of the Holy and Sacred Synod of the Church of the True Orthodox Christians of Greece, by Archpriest Eugene Tombros. Athens, January 1962.

The Calendar Change, by Polycarp, Bishop of Diauleia; Athens, 1947.

Concerning the Secular Calendar (Hemerologion) and the Festal Calendar (Heortologion), by Callistus, Bishop of Corinth, 1966.

An Answer to An Epistolary Study, by the Zealot Fathers of the Holy Mountain, Lycobrysis, Attica, 1969.

An Epistolary Study, by Alexander Kalomiros; (see *The Voice of Orthodoxy*).

Concerning the Unity of the Orthodox in the Feasts and the 'Common Pascha,' by Paul, a Monk of the Holy Sepulcher in Jerusalem, 1970.

French Sources:

Calendrier Ecclesiastique Permanent, edite par la Mission Orthodoxe de Pekinen 1929.

Lettre ouverte a tous les fideles de l'Eglise du Christ qui gardent fidelement le calendrier orthodoxe et les Traditions de l'Eglise Une, Sainte, Catholique et Apostolique. Par S. E. Mgr. Innocent, Archeveque de Pekin en 1929.